W indows 10 Primer

Mik

SS®

Windows 10 Primer: What to Expect from Microsoft's New Operating System

ISBN-13 (pbk): 978-1-4842-1047-5

ISBN-13 (electronic): 978-1-4842-1046-8

Managing Director: Welmoed Spahr
Lead Editor: Gwenan Spearing
Technical Reviewer: Kathleen Anderson
Editorial Board: Steve Anglin, Gary Cornell, Louise Corrigan, James T. DeWolf,
	Jonathan Gennick, Robert Hutchinson, Michelle Lowman, James Markham,
	Matthew Moodie, Susan McDermott, Jeffrey Pepper, Douglas Pundick,
	Dominic Shakeshaft, Gwenan Spearing, Matt Wade, Steve Weiss
Coordinating Editor: Melissa Maldonado
Copy Editor: April Rondeau
Compositor: SPi Global
Indexer: SPi Global
Artist: SPi Global

Distributed to the book trade worldwide by Springer Science+Business Media New York, 233 Spring Street, 6th Floor, New York, NY 10013. Phone 1-800-SPRINGER, fax (201) 348-4505, e-mail orders-ny@springer-sbm.com, or visit www.springeronline.com. Apress Media, LLC is a California LLC and the sole member (owner) is Springer Science + Business Media Finance Inc (SSBM Finance Inc). SSBM Finance Inc is a Delaware corporation.

For information on translations, please e-mail rights@apress.com, or visit www.apress.com.

Apress and friends of ED books may be purchased in bulk for academic, corporate, or promotional use. eBook versions and licenses are also available for most titles. For more information, reference our Special Bulk Sales–eBook Licensing web page at www.apress.com/bulk-sales.

Any source code or other supplementary material referenced by the author in this text is available to readers at www.apress.com. For detailed information about how to locate your book's source code, go to www.apress.com/source-code/.

For Lawrence Hall (1942–2014)
Friend, Confidant, and always an IT Pro

Contents at a Glance

Contents

About the Author

Mike Halsey is a Microsoft MVP (Most Valuable Professional) awardee and the author of many Windows books, including the forthcoming *Beginning Windows 10* and *Windows 10 Troubleshooting* from Apress. They're great books that he believes would make excellent Christmas presents!

Mike gives many talks about Windows subjects ranging from productivity to security and has been beta testing Windows versions since Vista. He makes help, how-to, and troubleshooting videos under the banner PC Support.tv. You can follow him on Facebook and Twitter @PCSupportTV, and you'll be able to watch his new Windows 10 productivity videos later this year at Windows.do.

About the Technical Reviewer

Kathleen Anderson was first honored with the Microsoft MVP award in October 2001. She has worked with FrontPage since 1997, with Expression Web since Version 1, and in the IT field for over thirty years. Kathleen recently retired from the State of Connecticut after 25 years of service, and has relocated to the beach in Oak Island, North Carolina. She served as the Core-CT Webmaster (http://www.core-ct.state.ct.us) and chaired the State of Connecticut's Committee on Web Site Accessibility. She owns a web design company, Spider Web Woman Designs (http://www.spiderwebwoman.com). She was a Technical Editor on Microsoft Expression Web 4 In Depth; Sams Teach Yourself Microsoft Expression Web 4, Second Edition; Expression Blend 4 Step by Step; and My Kindle Fire. She is known in some circles as the "FrontPage Database Wizard Queen" and in others as the "Accessibility Diva."

Introduction

Windows 10 is the most hotly anticipated version of Microsoft's desktop OS in some time, and the first in just as long that has received almost universal acclaim from users, enthusiasts, bloggers, and the media, so the pressure's on to deliver something that's both super-cool and feature-packed.

Fortunately for Microsoft, they're delivering both qualities in spades, which seems odd to this author, as I've been, several times, to the surprisingly ordinary building in which it is being written, and shared coffee with some of the people who are bringing the magic to life. You might be surprised to hear that the Windows development team is not a vast army of programmers, but rather a smaller and select team of quite exceptional people who rarely get any of the praise they deserve.

There's simply so much that's new and improved stuffed into Windows 10 that it's a wonder these programmers ever get any sleep, or any time with their friends and family. Yet, time off they do indeed get, and despite the selfish needs of friends, family, spouses, and children outside of Microsoft, a fantastic operating system is being written.

It's not finished yet, though. As I write this introduction, pressure is piling on Microsoft to release more frequent beta builds of the OS, and it's clear from leaks and news stories that there's an awful long way to go yet.

Sooner or later, though, this operating system will be finished, and it will be spectacular and packed so full of features that you may never find them all (not unless you buy my *Beginning Windows 10* and *Windows 10 Troubleshooting* books later this year, anyway). In this book, though, I hope to get you started, excited, and enthused about what Windows 10 will be able to do for you, your family, and your business.

CHAPTER 1

■ ■ ■

Introducing Windows 10

First unveiled to the world in April 2014 at Microsoft's BUILD conference, Windows 10 is the seventeenth version of Microsoft's desktop operating system, and the ninth version of the business-focused NT kernel. There, we got the naming question out of the way early on.

Windows 10 follows Windows 8.1, which suffered from poor take-up from many consumers because of criticism of its "modern" touch-friendly user interface and what was a perceived focus away from the desktop toward smaller, tablet- and hybrid-style devices.

In the business space, Windows 8 and 8.1 were always likely to be skipped, as large businesses only like to upgrade their desktop operating systems every two Windows versions and, as Windows 8 was being launched, many were only beginning deployments of Windows 7.

It's often been said that Windows releases are rather like *Star Trek* movies, in that only every other one is great. Both Windows XP and Windows 7 launched to enormous rapture and fanfare, gaining plaudits around the world and building armies of loyal fans. The releases between these, however—Vista and Windows 8—despite both being major updates to the OS, were less well received. Vista was seen to be slow and resource-hungry, and Windows 8 was seen to be not very good on the desktop.

With Windows 10, Microsoft has sought to address all of the concerns people have had, not just about Windows 8, but about Windows in general. More than this, however, the company has looked in detail at what people liked most about Windows XP and Windows 7 and worked to ensure that people get an experience with Windows 10 that they'll both feel comfortable with and enjoy. Indeed, in November 2014 I spoke to some senior members of the Windows product team and told them that Windows 10 would be successful simply because, like XP and Windows 7, they'd made it blue.

So let's return to the name, as many people have wondered why Microsoft made the jump from Windows 8.1 to Windows 10. This new operating system is intended to be the last major version of the Windows OS. This doesn't mean it will be going away, but rather, like Apple did with their OS X desktop operating system, it won't again be receiving the kind of major updates we saw in Windows 8.

1

▓ **Note**   The minimum hardware specification Microsoft have detailed for a PC capable of running Windows 10 is a processor running at 1GHz or faster, a minimum 1GB RAM (2GB for the 64-bit version of Windows 10), at least 16GB free storage for the OS, and graphics that support DirectX 9 or later. Not all 1GHz+ processors will be compatible however, you should check your processor specifications to see if it supports the PAE, NX and SSE2 standards (all of which are required by Windows 10).

Windows 10 will also be Microsoft's first truly cross-platform operating system, running on everything from desktops, laptops, and tablets down to phones, the Xbox One, and Internet of Things (IoT) devices, and upwards to their new Surface Hub and Holographic headset, HoloLens (see Figure 1-1).

Figure 1-1. *One Windows for all your devices*

For such a major release, and for the final major release of Windows, the number 9 just didn't sound major enough, and, frankly, it would have been an odd number to finish on. The other alternative, just calling the OS "Windows," might have opened Microsoft to litigation and copyright claims in some markets in the way that happened with their SkyDrive cloud backup service in 2014. SkyDrive was eventually renamed OneDrive, but it would be harder to do this with Windows should litigation arise. And so Windows 10 it had to be.

The final release of Windows 10 will be out later in 2015, but for now we've got a beta Technical Preview release, and a lot of questions. That's what this book is for—to guide you through everything that's new, updated, or removed in Windows 10, answering the questions you have of how it will affect you, how it can aid productivity, how it will be more secure and robust, and so on.

By the time of the second major Technical Preview release in January 2015, there were more than 1.7 million people signed up with the Windows Insiders beta program, and there was a great deal of excitement and goodwill toward Microsoft's new OS.

This is still a beta product, however, designed by a team of extremely talented engineers in a building in Redmond, Washington (see Figure 1-2). This means that as you read this book, things will still be changing, and the final release will differ slightly from the screenshots and information you read here.

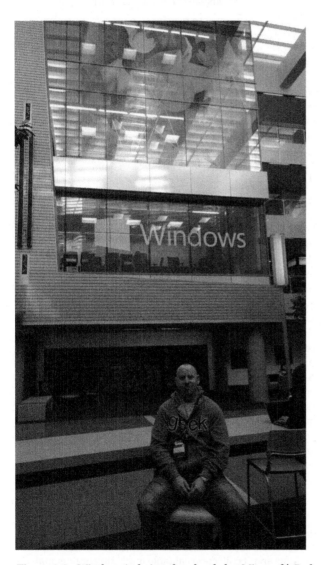

Figure 1-2. *Windows is designed and coded at Microsoft's Redmond Campus*

This isn't to say that we don't already know a great deal about what the final release will bring, and it's these details that I'll be sharing with you in this book.

■ **Note** You can download the Windows 10 Technical Preview at `https://insider.windows.com`. Please remember that this operating system is not finished and will be missing features and will be unstable on some hardware.

Microsoft's Three Areas of Focus

I've mentioned already that Microsoft wanted to achieve several things with Windows 10. In addition to pushing the Windows paradigm forward, they wanted to ensure that anybody moving to the OS from XP or Windows 7 would have a familiar and comfortable experience. To achieve these goals, they set themselves three areas of focus.

Mobility of Experience

Windows 8 set the goal of getting the user interface out of the way. The design brief for that OS was that your PC experience should be all about the content in your apps and not what's called the window furniture. This led to some issues of discoverability for UI features, such as the charms and the app menu bar.

Windows 10 is reversing this, but not completely. Options and menus are much more easily discovered in the new OS—indeed, they're exactly where you might expect to find them—but extra focus has been placed on getting the technology out of the way.

There is a great deal of clever and innovative technology in Windows 10, including features like OneDrive, Cortana, and Continuum, all of which will be detailed in the coming chapters. Microsoft doesn't want users to have to wade through myriad controls and settings just to be able to configure the OS and their apps to operate the way they want.

This is a good area to focus on when you think about it, as the number of tools, utilities, and features in the OS number in the hundreds, and the configuration options in the thousands or perhaps even the hundreds of thousands. Allowing people to focus on the content of their documents or web pages is an excellent place to begin.

In addition, Microsoft wants people's experience of Windows 10 to be the same across whichever device they use. This could be a desktop PC, a tablet, phone, or the Xbox. Each of these devices will synchronize with each other in new and clever ways, and Microsoft doesn't want people to have to learn how to use multiple interfaces and controls.

Trust

One of the biggest issues people have with technology in the twenty-first century is trust. How do we know that our devices are secure and that our files and data are safe? How do we know that the OS and our apps aren't collecting valuable marketing or personal data about us, and then broadcasting that to companies or even making it available to governments and security agencies?

Microsoft is emphasizing with Windows 10 that the user is firmly in control of their own privacy, and this begins at the installation stage, where you're asked what you want to share with Microsoft (see Figure 1-3) by bringing to the fore the privacy settings that people may otherwise fail to find after Windows is installed.

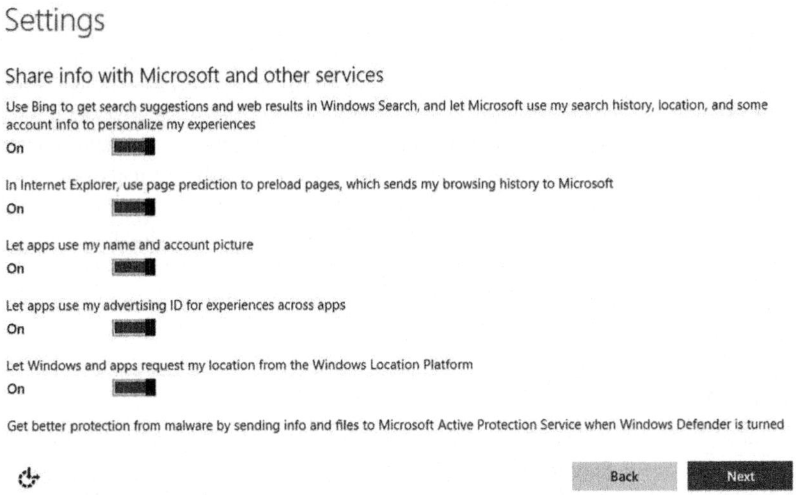

Settings

Share info with Microsoft and other services

Use Bing to get search suggestions and web results in Windows Search, and let Microsoft use my search history, location, and some account info to personalize my experiences

On

In Internet Explorer, use page prediction to preload pages, which sends my browsing history to Microsoft

On

Let apps use my name and account picture

On

Let apps use my advertising ID for experiences across apps

On

Let Windows and apps request my location from the Windows Location Platform

On

Get better protection from malware by sending info and files to Microsoft Active Protection Service when Windows Defender is turned

Back   Next

Figure 1-3. Privacy choices begin when you install Windows 10

The Cortana personal assistant can collect details about you, including your likes, location, friends, and more, in order to assist you day to day. All of this can be disabled if you don't wish the data to be stored, however. This focus on putting the user clearly and transparently in control of their data can be seen throughout the Windows 10 Technical Preview, and it will be welcomed by many around the world.

Additionally, new security features will help protect your files, data, and personal information from theft by unscrupulous individuals wishing to exploit you, and end-to-end encryption over company networks and the Internet can minimize the available surface for malware and hacking attacks.

Natural Interaction

Because Windows 10 will be the last major version of the OS, it needs to be forward-looking. We've used keyboards and mice to interact with our PCs since the advent of the computer, and they're still the most common way to interact today.

Windows has supported handwriting recognition for many years, however, and anybody who regularly uses OneNote on a Microsoft Surface Pro 3 will likely attest to how accurate and helpful it can be.

Speech recognition is also improving significantly, and anybody who's used Cortana on their Windows Phone will know how useful it can be to be able to dictate emails, text messages, reminders, and more. Then there's gesture control, both for tablet and hybrid devices, and also used in a way by Microsoft's Kinect gaming sensor.

However you want to interact with Windows 10, and whatever device it is done on, be this a desktop PC, tablet, or HoloLens headset, the OS includes controls that are natural and intuitive to use, and that have been refined by Microsoft over many years.

Lastly, there's vision. It's very common for PCs, especially laptops and tablets, to come with forward-facing cameras, and so it seems right that Microsoft also allows you to control your PC with a smile and a wave.

Above and beyond all else, these many input and control methods make Windows more accessible for a broader range of people. It's not just those with physical disabilities who can have trouble interacting with a PC. Those with even minor motor or vision problems, such as nearsightedness, and the very young can experience difficulty. Expanding the range of interaction methods helps future-proof the OS as we all get older and hungrier for technology and a connection to the Internet.

The Big Questions

Naturally, people are asking a lot of questions about Windows 10, which also means there are a lot of inaccurate answers being provided, even on some of the most popular technology blogs. Let's deal with these questions one by one and weed out the facts from the fiction. What follows are the most common questions being asked by both individual consumers and businesses about Windows 10.

Pricing and Availability

There's no formal release date for Windows 10 other than "the second half of 2015," and no pricing has been announced either. What has been said is that for PC users running up-to-date copies of Windows 7 and Windows 8.1, the upgrade to Windows 10 will be *free* for the first twelve months of the life of the new OS.

There has been some confusion about this, with a few bloggers speculating that after this introductory period users will have to pay a charge or even a regular subscription to use their own PCs. So let's get the first piece of misinformation out of the way. Free means free! If you upgrade your copy of Windows 7 or Windows 8.1 during the first twelve months after Windows 10 is released, you will *never* again have to pay a fee to use Windows 10 on that PC. This includes all major updates to Windows 10, all of which will also be free.

If you purchase a new PC, you will also be purchasing a new copy of Windows 10 with it, and should you upgrade a PC from Windows XP or Windows Vista, you will need to purchase a download or retail copy of the OS.

Again, we don't know what pricing will be. At their January 2015 event, Microsoft stated that they just haven't decided on pricing yet. When Windows 8 launched, however, there were discounted offers available for those purchasing a copy of the OS early, and it is Microsoft's intention to have as many PC users as possible switch to Windows 10 as quickly as possible.

It's entirely likely then that discounts will be available for XP and Vista users, but only for a limited time of perhaps a month or so. These are questions we simply don't have any answers to yet, but Microsoft is very unlikely to place barriers in the way to upgrading.

Upgrading from Windows 7 or Windows 8.1

If you are currently using Windows 7 or Windows 8.1 you will be able to upgrade for free when Windows 10 is released. Indeed, if you have already upgraded to the Windows 10 Technical Preview from one of these operating systems you will also be able to upgrade to the final version of the OS for *free*.

The upgrade will be available several different ways to ensure that the maximum number of people will be able to take advantage of it. If you subscribe to a service such as Microsoft's Developer Network (MSDN), you will be able to download a full ISO image file for the final version, which can be mounted inside Windows or burned to a DVD. Running *Setup* from within this ISO file will allow you to upgrade to Windows 10.

▪ **Note**   Windows 8.1 allows you to natively mount an ISO file so that it can be accessed as if it were a hard disk. Right-click on the file and select Mount from the options that appear.

Perhaps more useful as well as easier to use, the Windows 10 upgrade will also be the first time Microsoft has released an operating system through Windows Update. Normally a mechanism for downloading and installing security and stability patches and service packs, Windows Update has a name that naturally implies that it ought to be possible to use it to update Windows. Indeed, this will be the case, as Windows 10 will appear as an optional update for users of Windows 7 and Windows 8.1 upon its release.

The final way to upgrade to Windows 10 is being used by Insiders to install the Technical Preview, and this is a small install file that can be downloaded manually from the Microsoft website. It's not yet known if the free update will be available in this form, though it is very likely that online purchases of the OS will come with both the ISO file and the small downloader.

Upgrading your PC from Windows 7 and Windows 8.1 will allow you to keep everything in place: your files, settings, and all your apps and desktop programs. Microsoft has worked hard to ensure this is the case.

The upgrade process also includes a downgrade option for the first time, enabling you to roll back to your previous copy of Windows as though Windows 10 were never there, should you want to do this.

Upgrading from Windows RT

If you are using a Windows RT device such as Microsoft's Surface RT or Surface 2 tablets, you will also be able to upgrade to Windows 10 on its release, though the overall experience might be slightly different for you.

Microsoft has yet to explain how the Windows 10 experience for Windows RT devices, as well as some lower-end Windows Phone handsets, will be different. We do know, however, that small Windows 10 devices, those with screens of eight inches or less, will come with touch-enabled versions of Microsoft Outlook, Word, Excel, and PowerPoint. These apps will be available to purchase in the Windows Store for other devices and will likely be free with some Office 365 subscriptions.

This is speculation at this point, but it is entirely likely that these touch versions of Office will replace the desktop editions in Windows RT, as Microsoft has said that Windows devices with screens of eight inches or less won't have a desktop. This is also likely to extend to RT-based devices.

Upgrading from XP or Vista

There is no direct upgrade path from Windows XP or Windows Vista, and Microsoft has not yet commented on whether you will be able to perform an in-place upgrade or a clean installation of Windows 10.

When Windows 8 was released it was possible to upgrade in place from Vista, but not to keep your apps, just your settings and files. It's likely that running the installer from within Windows Vista will replicate that behavior, so you will need to reinstall your programs and configure your settings after Windows 10 is installed.

Windows XP is an unknown at this stage, but the upgrade process to Windows 8 would only allow you to keep your personal files. Should an in-place upgrade for Windows XP be supported, this will still be the case. This is because the core architecture of XP is fundamentally different from that of Microsoft's modern operating systems, and the settings for the OS are also extremely different.

Windows 10 on New PCs

If you purchase a new PC from the release date of the OS onwards, you will get a full copy of Windows 10 installed on it. This won't be a free copy, but instead will be included in the cost of the PC hardware.

This could be either a clean copy of the OS or a version modified by the OEM (Original Equipment Manufacturer) that built the PC. OEM copies of Windows are tied to particular hardware and cannot be moved to different PCs, unlike clean copies downloaded from Microsoft or purchased in retail stores, which Microsoft allows you to move to a different PC should yours die.

Software Assurance

Enterprise customers who subscribe to Microsoft's Software Assurance program will be unaffected. ISO image files for Windows 10 will be available to download and install from the day the operating system hits RTM (Release to Manufacturing), which is roughly 30 days before the retail release.

Microsoft has said that Software Assurance customers will not qualify for the free upgrade to Windows 10 even if their computers are running Windows 7 or Windows 8.1, as the Enterprise edition will not be included in the offer.

Upgrading from Windows Phone 8.1 and Xbox

Microsoft has said that all users of Windows Phone 8.1 will be able to get a free upgrade to Windows 10 for Phones, but there is a caveat. Some cellular networks have decided not to further support some phone models, and this can include ones that can get Windows 10.

For cellular networks that are supporting the upgrade, you can expect the rollout to begin at the time of Windows 10's retail release, and then run for a period of months afterwards, so not all phones will get the upgrade immediately. This happens because the networks and handset manufacturers need to be certain that any OS update will be fully compatible with their handsets and their own apps, and they need time to test the OS and update any apps as necessary.

If you are not already using Windows Phone 8.1, and updates are not available, you will not be able to upgrade your handset to Windows 10. That is, unless you download the *Preview for Developers* app, from http://pcs.tv/1uGTqB9, and use it to create a free app developer account with Microsoft.

This allows you to get free OS updates directly from Microsoft, bypassing the cellular networks altogether. By doing this, any handset that's capable of running Windows Phone 8.1 will be able to upgrade to Windows 10.

Anybody with an Xbox One console will get the upgrade automatically on its release. The Xbox 360 console will not be upgraded to Windows 10.

What Else Do You Need to Know?

Despite the answers to the most common questions being relatively straightforward, not everything about upgrading or migrating to Windows 10 is as simple, and there are a few issues and features of which you'll probably want to be aware before you take the plunge.

Upgrading and the Storage Space Problem

This talk of Windows Phones does raise a prickly subject, that of available storage space. Anybody with a lower-cost Windows Phone might already have experienced problems trying to install OS updates where not enough free space is available on the handset.

If your phone has a Micro SD card slot and a card inserted, you can open *Settings* and then *Storage Sense* to change the default storage location for files, music, photos, and videos and the default install location for apps.

A minimum amount of storage space, as yet undetermined, will be required for the upgrade, and you may have to uninstall some apps to free up enough space.

The problem will similarly affect small Windows 8.1 tablets, which have very limited amounts of storage, such as just 16GB or 32GB. Once you have some apps installed the amount of available space can drop sharply.

The Windows 10 upgrade process requires 5GB of free space if you install from Windows update, or 8GB if you download the ISO file and install from that. You may need to uninstall apps or perform a disk cleanup to free up the necessary space. Disk cleanup, however, doesn't delete all the settings and configuration files for apps that can build up over a period of time.

Should this be the case, in PC Settings, in the Update and Recovery section, you can Refresh or Reset your tablet, which will free up the necessary space to allow you to install Windows 10.

Additionally, Windows 10 includes a roll-back feature, which you can use to revert to the operating system version you had on your PC before Windows 10 was installed. This will use additional space in PCs with good-sized hard disks, but can be removed in the Disk Cleanup tool by clicking the "Clean up system files" button and checking the "Previous Windows Installation(s)" option.

Rolling Back Windows 10

Let's look now in more detail at the new feature that allows you to roll back the OS to the version of Windows you were using before, be this Windows 7 or Windows 8.

■ **Note**   Because of the fundamental architectural differences between Windows 10, Vista, and Windows XP, it is unlikely that this option will be available for people who have upgraded in place from those earlier versions of Windows.

This feature can be found in the new Settings panel, which will amalgamate the Control Panel and Windows 8.1's PC Settings into a single location. You can launch Settings from the Start menu, where it is listed in the Places section (more on the Start menu in Chapter 4).

In Settings, click Update and Recovery and then Recovery for the option to "Go back to a previous version of Windows" (see Figure 1-4).

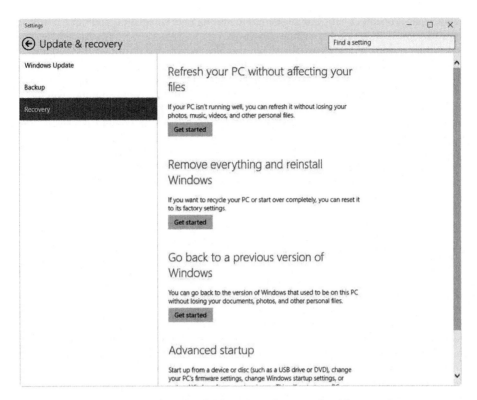

Figure 1-4. *You can roll back to Windows 7 or Windows 8.1 should you wish*

Why would you want to do this? You may find that some piece of software or hardware that is critical to your work is fundamentally incompatible with Windows 10. Or you may just decide that you don't like the OS.

▓ **Note** It's worth noting here that Windows 7 will be completely out of support in 2020, just five short years from now. If you are still using Windows 7 at that time, there will be no more security and stability patches for the OS, and it will become a target for malware writers and hackers.

The Improved Installation and Updating Experience

If you are upgrading to Windows 10, however, you'll be delighted to hear that the upgrade experience has been dramatically improved.

On my own PC, on which I'm writing this book, I have huge volumes of Microsoft and third-party software installed, including Microsoft Office, Adobe Creative Cloud,

Sony Vegas Pro Suite, a couple of big games including Elite Dangerous, and more besides; my programs folders stand at a whopping 95GB.

With previous Windows installs, the more software you had the longer the upgrade process would take, as everything was migrated across. This still might be the case when upgrading from some Windows 7 systems, and this is a question that Microsoft has not yet addressed, but in Windows 8 the in-place upgrade takes around twenty minutes whether you have a lot of software already installed or not.

Additionally, major updates to Windows 10 in the future won't require long waits or even huge downloads. Microsoft is building a new updating system into Windows 10 so that only the components that require updating are downloaded and installed, and everything that doesn't need to be touched is left alone.

The upshot of this is that the full update for a system might be 3GB in size, but less than 1GB of that update is actually downloaded and installed, as the other 2GB of files would remain the same anyway.

Windows 10, Different by Device

Of the questions that are as yet unanswered about Windows 10, one of the most significant is Microsoft's statement that the full Windows 10 experience will not be available on every device that runs the OS.

In this they have pointed to tablets that are currently running Windows RT and some low-cost Windows Phones. What has been said is that "upgraded hardware" would be required for some features and as it's not possible to upgrade the hardware in tablets and smartphones, these features will simply not be available on all devices.

It's reasonable to speculate that this will include some of the more graphics-intensive features such as DirectX 12. The core Windows 10 experience is unlikely to change, nor is the synchronization with OneDrive. Cortana could be one of the features listed, however, depending on the amount of processing power required, and some additional features that have yet to be announced may require specific hardware to function.

No Desktop on Smaller PCs

One of the contentious issues facing PC users is the matter of the desktop. On Windows RT-based devices the desktop serves little purpose, as these machines' ARM processors won't run win32 desktop applications anyway. You can access specially-written desktop versions of Outlook, Word, Excel, and Powerpoint and access the Control Panel, but that's about it.

Other small tablets running Windows 8 or Windows 8 Pro that have an HDMI or other video output can be plugged into an external monitor so as to use the desktop with a full Bluetooth keyboard and mouse.

Microsoft has said that on devices with an eight-inch screen or smaller there will be *no* desktop in Windows 10 at all, so you'll only be able to run Universal apps from the Windows Store, and only full screen or side by side. This may affect your buying decisions for future Windows hardware—for example, you might purchase a ten-inch tablet instead—and it's an important consideration for Windows 10 users.

Summary

There are a lot of questions about Windows 10, especially when it comes to pricing, availability, and compatibility, and hopefully I've answered some of your most pressing ones here.

That aside, the real excitement around Windows 10 is in its new features for home users, businesses, and gamers, and in the next chapter I'll talk in depth about each one and explain what they will mean to you and how they can improve your PC experience and productivity.

■ ■ ■

CHAPTER 2

New and Improved Features in Windows 10

Every version of Windows comes with new features: Windows 95 introduced the Start Menu; Windows XP saw the OS move to the much more stable NT kernel as well as brought in major refinements to the user interface; Vista came with some major changes, including a wholesale kernel upgrade, a new hardware driver model, and user account control; Windows 7 introduced aero glass, snap, the new Taskbar, and the Action Center; and Windows 8 introduced the Start Screen, Modern apps, and the addition of ARM processor support.

Windows 10 is no different, and the list of new and improved features is both long and significant. Indeed, it can safely be said that the list of new features is the greatest that's been seen in any Windows release thus far, and almost the entire focus is being placed firmly on productivity.

I'm not going to detail every improved feature and new addition in this chapter, as many of them fall into categories that are much better detailed elsewhere in this book under more specific categories, such as end-user desktop features or business-specific features. There are some major changes and additions, however, that need to be detailed on their own, and in this chapter I'll look at them in no particular order.

Cortana

Okay, I lied! I'm hugely excited about the inclusion of Cortana in Windows 10, and thus it has to be detailed first. Cortana is Microsoft's answer to Apple's Siri and Google Now, in that it's a personal digital assistant (originally to be called Judy, so I'm told, though its beta name, taken from the AI computer in the Halo series of Xbox games, was so popular with Windows Phone testers that Microsoft kept it).

Cortana first appeared in Windows Phone 8.1 in 2014 and has been slowly rolling out to countries worldwide. Cortana does much more than answer basic search queries and provide the latest news and weather updates. Already ahead of Apple's Siri and Google Now, Cortana can provide recipes and dietary information, automatically follow parcel tracking information you've been emailed, and monitor flights and other travel methods. She (I hate calling Cortana "It") can set and modify reminders and calendar appointments, as well as set reminders based on location, such as when you get home or when you're next in the city center. She can provide idle chit chat, sing you songs, tell you jokes, and even speak Klingon.

This is the state of Cortana today, and her functionality is being expanded all the time with new features, some of which (such as being able to bark Klingon at you) aren't actively promoted but were simply found accidentally by users.

"So how does all of this help me become more productive on the desktop?" you ask. You might, for example, work in a busy office where talking to your PC is never going to be effective, or your PC might not even have a microphone, or you may just be uncomfortable with the prospect of striking up a conversation with the thing.

Typing requests and commands into Cortana brings the same functionality as speaking to her, and being able to quickly ask what appointments you have in the coming week, or to have her reschedule your 3 o'clock appointment for 5, or to dictate to her an email for Sue in Accounts can save valuable time.

Cortana can be found next to the Windows icon on the Windows 10 desktop Taskbar (see Figure 2-1), and will also likely be a Start Screen icon on tablets in the final release.

Figure 2-1. *Cortana's icon is a circle and is located next to the Windows button on the Taskbar*

▓ **Note** It's likely that Cortana will not be available in every country on Windows 10's launch, and this is certainly the case with the technical preview. If Cortana is not available to you yet, you will instead see a search (magnifying glass) icon next to the Windows icon.

When you open Cortana you will be presented with information that's relevant to you (see Figure 2-2). An *Ask me anything* box at the bottom of her window is where you can type commands, search requests, and more, and next to this is a microphone icon that you can click to enable you to speak to her.

Figure 2-2. By default, Cortana will show you information that's relevant to you

You will also be able to activate Cortana by simply saying *Hey, Cortana* while at your computer, though with this feature also reported to be coming to Windows 10 for Phones it remains to be seen how it'll work should you also have your phone on your desk when you say this.

I want to deal with search first in Cortana, as the search feature that Cortana brings to Windows is a significant improvement over previous Windows versions. When typing into the *Ask me anything* box, search results are immediately displayed and will include installed apps and win32 desktop programs, photos, music, video, documents, emails, settings, and websites (see Figure 2-3).

Figure 2-3. *Search responds immediately when typing into Cortana*

You can click any item in these search results to open it, or, alternatively, clicking *Search my stuff* (or just pressing the Enter key) will display a more detailed contextual search box (see Figure 2-4).

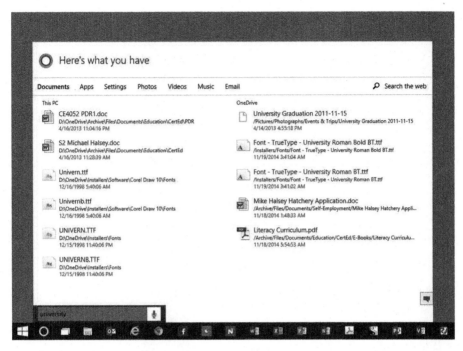

Figure 2-4. *Search my stuff provides a more detailed, contextual search*

It's with this contextual search box that the true power of search in Windows 10 is revealed. The box contains a tabbed interface, allowing you to easily and quickly switch your search between documents, apps, settings, photos, videos, music, email, and the Internet.

This search facility combines those found in File Explorer and the Start Menu and improves on both while greatly simplifying the overall process.

Managing Cortana's Settings and Privacy

You can manage Cortana's settings and options very easily by clicking the hamburger icon (so called because it consists of three horizontal lines) in the top left of Cortana's window. Here you can manage any reminders you have set (see Figure 2-5) and any places you want Cortana to know about (should you be using a laptop or tablet), as well as change overall settings, such as allowing Cortana to call you by your name and even turning the feature off altogether.

Figure 2-5. Cortana's options are easy to find and access

In this age of personal privacy, data protection, and government spying, some of you might be uncomfortable with Cortana having access to all of your emails and other personal information. Cortana is designed to soak up all this information and learn more about you over time to make her more effective.

One of Microsoft's three pillars for Windows 10 was putting the user firmly in control of their own data and their own privacy, and Cortana is no exception. The information you choose to share about yourself is managed in Cortana's *Notebook* (see Figure 2-6).

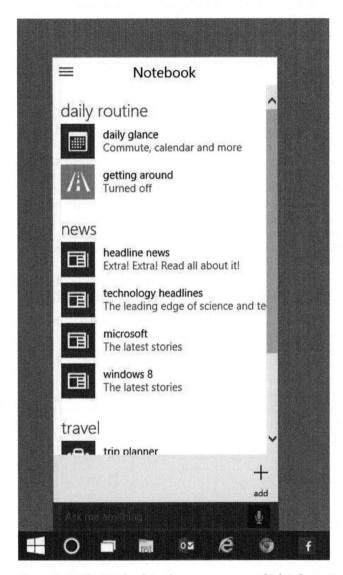

Figure 2-6. *The Notebook is where you manage which information you share*

Here, you can manage all the data that Cortana stores about you, including your news preferences, calendar access, whether Cortana is allowed to read your emails for parcel tracking and flight details, and much more besides.

The Notebook isn't just about your privacy, however; adding and refining the information that's here can help Cortana provide you with more relevant news and information, thus reducing the need to use news and weather apps or websites.

That Syncing Feeling

Those of you who have been using Windows 8.1 with a Microsoft account will likely be used to the OS syncing your settings and preferences between PCs. For example, if you purchase a new tablet and log in using the same Microsoft Account ID that you use on your desktop, you'll see your Start Screen and apps are just as they are on that first machine.

Syncing is being extended even further in Windows 10, allowing Cortana on your different PCs, tablets, and phone so as to share information with one another. This includes your reminders, so you'll never miss one just because you happen to be away from the PC you set it on, and more besides.

Syncing between different devices can be managed both from within Cortana herself and from the new *All Settings* panel, which replaces the Control Panel and PC Settings.

Managing Different Form Factors with Continuum

One of the biggest criticisms of Windows 8 was that people found the transition from the Start Screen to the Desktop "jarring." Windows 8.1 made some effort to reduce this by allowing your desktop wallpaper to be used for the Start Screen, but Windows 10 handles things much more effectively through the use of a new feature called Continuum.

Continuum works in two separate ways: first, it allows you to resize the Start Menu between its desktop and full-screen options (see the icon in the top right of the Start Menu in Figure 2-7), and, second, it allows you to automatically switch between desktop and full-screen modes on convertible devices.

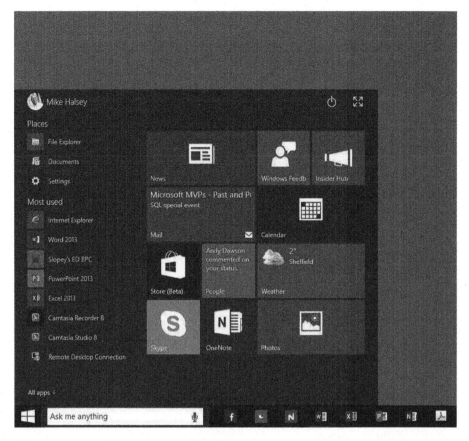

Figure 2-7. *One click can resize the Start Menu*

If you are using a convertible laptop, such as the Lenovo Yoga, and you switch the PC into its tablet form-factor, then a system tray notification will be displayed asking if you wish to switch to full-screen mode (along with a *don't ask me this again* check box).

Allowing this change will automatically switch all your apps and the Start Menu to full-screen mode, along with making some additional changes, such as spacing out some UI elements to make them easier to hit with a finger.

Continuum also works with tablets that have Bluetooth keyboards attached, and you can switch manually between desktop and tablet modes in the All Settings panel (it is expected that a notification area button will also be in the final release).

The Notification Center

Speaking of the new Notification Center, you may already be familiar with these in Windows Phone 8.1 as well as on other smartphone platforms, such as Android and iOS, and even on the Apple OS X desktop. Well, now the Notification Center has come to Windows.

Notifications in Windows have long suffered from two problems. First, with Windows XP people complained that notifications appeared far too often and were generally annoying. The second problem was that each notification would only appear for a few seconds before disappearing forever.

With Windows 7, Microsoft sought to partially rectify this problem by including some notifications in the new Action Center. This included security and troubleshooting alerts, but didn't go so far as to add notifications for appointments, email, and the like.

Well, the Action Center has been removed from the Taskbar with Windows 10 and has been replaced by the new Notification Center (see Figure 2-8).

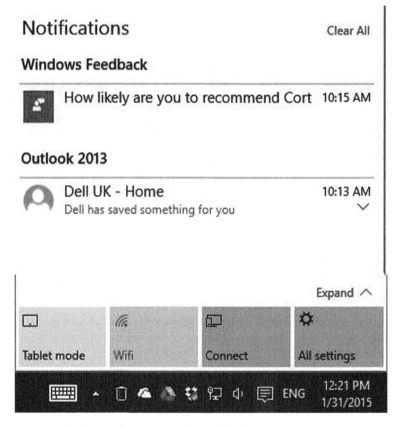

Figure 2-8. *The Windows 10 Notification Center*

It is here that a list of all your notifications will appear, and stay, until cleared manually by yourself or until pushed aside should the list become full. Each notification in the final release of Windows 10 will respond in different ways to various actions, including being dismissed by a swipe to the right.

At the bottom of the notification center are quick-link buttons that perform specific tasks. In Figure 2-8 these include a button to activate the Continuum feature that switches between desktop and tablet modes, a Wi-Fi on/off button, a network connection button, and a quick link to the new All Settings panel.

Just as with Windows Phone 8.1, these buttons will be configurable in the final release of Windows 10 and are expected to include the features already found in the phone OS, such as Quiet Hours to hide notifications and silence alarms, alongside PC-specific options such as toggling GPS and location services or turning Cortana on and off.

Windows 10 will still permit *Toast* notifications to appear on your screen, so called because they "pop up," and these will appear in the bottom right of your screen. Should you choose to turn toasts off for specific apps, however, such as those for your email client, you will still be able to get notifications in the new Notification Center.

You can open the Notification Center by clicking its icon on the Taskbar or by swiping inwards from the right of your screen, the action that used to display the now removed Charms.

Integrating Your PC(s) and Phone

Do you remember the days when a PC was stand-alone machine, and if you wanted to move files to another PC you had to copy them to removable storage such as a CD or floppy disk first?

Back then, if you got a new PC you had to change all your settings manually on the new machine, or reprogram all your phone numbers into a new phone. In fact, it's only in the last few years that this has changed, and it all started with Windows 8.

Some smartphone operating systems, such as iOS, would already allow you to back up your phone's settings so that if you got a new phone, perhaps because yours broke, you could reinstate those settings quickly and easily.

There were also web browsers such as Google Chrome that would allow you to synchronize your favorites between different PCs.

Windows 8 took things a step further, however, by allowing you to synchronize your Start Screen color and layout, including installed apps, desktop color-scheme, ease of access settings, Internet Favorites, and more between multiple PCs.

Windows 8.1 and Windows Phone 8.1 took this yet a step further, helping you to synchronize website usernames and passwords between PCs and phone.

Then there was the integration of Microsoft's cloud backup service, OneDrive, so that you could not only synchronize your files and documents between devices, but choose which ones were stored locally on each individual machine (useful for Ultrabooks and tablets with only small amounts of local storage).

Windows 10 takes this to the logical conclusion by allowing syncing of reminders and notification center items (including which ones have been dismissed).

As with Cortana, and indeed every aspect of Windows 10, you can control all aspects of the information that's synced in the All Settings panel (see Figure 2-9).

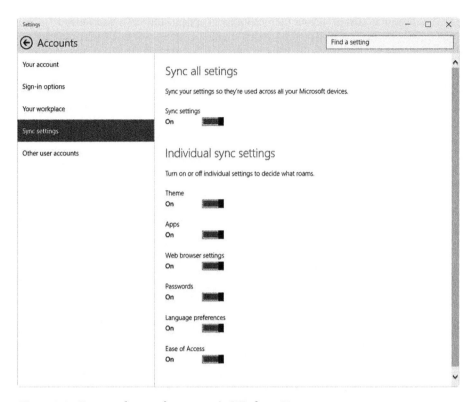

Figure 2-9. You can choose what to sync in WIndows 10

Microsoft Office for Windows 10

When Windows 8 launched with its modern app framework, many wondered when touch-enabled versions of Microsoft's Office suite would become available for the platform. Indeed, in the three years that followed, both iOS and Android versions of Word, Excel, PowerPoint, and Outlook appeared, first for a subscription charge and then for free. Throughout all this time, however, the only Microsoft Office program to get its own Modern app was OneNote.

As you might expect, this is being rectified with the launch of Windows 10 with Modern apps (now called Universal apps) available for the first time for Word (see Figure 2-10), Excel, PowerPoint, Outlook, and, once again, OneNote.

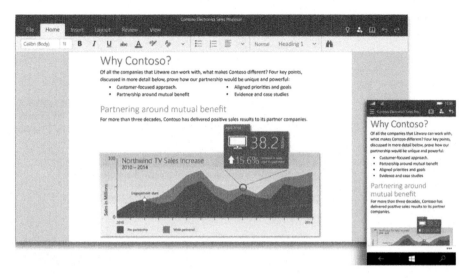

Figure 2-10. *The Microsoft Word universal app for WIndows 10 and Windows 10 for Phone*

There are still some unanswered questions about overall availability and pricing, however. Office is one of Microsoft's biggest earners, and their Office 365 subscription service proved conclusively that subscription-model software would work as an effective delivery and management method.

Microsoft has said that all Windows 10 devices with screens less than eight inches, which will include all phones and "phablets," will get these Office apps preinstalled for free.

It's very unlikely that users of Windows 10 tablets, laptops, and desktops with screens larger than eight inches will be unable to get the apps. Though pricing hasn't yet been discussed, it's entirely possible they will be free to install and use.

If you already have an Office 365 subscription, then chances are good that you will get the apps for free on all the devices on which you can use your Office 365 account, even if there is a charge in the Windows Store for the apps.

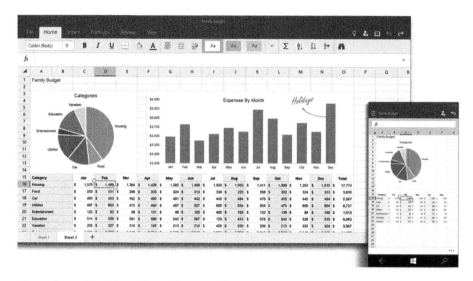

Figure 2-11. *The Microsoft Excel universal app*

Each Office app uses a trimmed version of the Office Ribbon interface, which was first seen in Office 2007, and each ribbon includes a subset of the functionality found in the full desktop versions of the apps.

In Windows 10 for Phones, the ribbon is condensed into a menu displayed by hitting the menu (three dots) icon in the bottom right of the screen.

The Office apps functionality is similar to that seen in the free web-based versions of these products, and the apps operate in a similar way. What I mean by this is that the web-based versions of Word, Excel, and PowerPoint display all aspects of the documents that are opened in them correctly, even if they don't natively support all of the features that control those aspects (such as commenting, for example).

Spartan!

Spartan is the new web browser with the cool name, or at least a cool beta name … for now. It's been reported that Microsoft has been considering several options for a final name, including Entourage, Elixa, Evo, Evex, Endeavor, and Edge, but that many Windows 10 Insiders favor the name Spartan (as do I, frankly). It could be the case that, as with Cortana, the beta name sticks.

So why would Microsoft bundle a brand new browser with Windows 10, and what does this mean for Internet Explorer, especially for businesses that rely on its compatibility with older plug-ins and intranet sites?

There has been much misinformation written on tech blogs about what Spartan means for IE users, so we should probably deal with this first.

While it's so far unclear whether IE will be included in the Home edition of Windows 10, it will definitely be included in the Pro and Enterprise editions, as many businesses simply can't live without it.

IE will not be available on Windows 10 devices with screens of eight inches or less. This is because Spartan will be replacing the Modern IE version from Windows 8.1, and devices with screens of eight inches or less won't support the desktop environment.

So what is Spartan? Simply put, Spartan is a modern, up-to-date Internet browser that supports all the latest web standards and that is built to be fast. Internet Explorer has lost significant ground to Mozilla Firefox and Google Chrome in recent years because its need to maintain compatibility with older websites, intranets, and plug-ins has made it slow and baggy.

Figure 2-12. *The new Spartan web browser*

Spartan won't be complexly stripped back, however. Microsoft has confirmed that it will support plug-ins, which is great news for people who use advert blockers or other utilities. It's not yet been stated whether these plug-ins will need to be created specifically for Spartan, as some have speculated that Microsoft may support plug-ins created for Google's Chrome browser.

Microsoft is aiming to make Spartan more than just a web browser, however. At their January 2015 Windows 10 event they showed off some of the features they'll be bringing to the browser. These include the ability to write or type notes on a web page and annotate it with highlights and drawn lines. These annotated pages can then be "locked" so that their content won't update as the website changes, and can be shared easily with other people.

Full details of Spartan are thin on the ground as I write this, and a public build currently isn't available. We can be reasonably certain that the note-taking and annotation facilities in the browser won't be the last of the new features.

What we do know is that the new rendering engine for the browser is built into the current version of IE in the Windows 10 Technical Preview, and that you can turn it on by typing **about:flags** into the address bar and activating *Enable Experimental Web Platform Features*. Browser speed tests have already been performed on this new, unfinished rendering engine and it's shown in some tests to be the fastest browser-rendering engine currently available.

Dawn of the Universal App

One of the biggest complaints about the app store in Windows 8.1 is that you had to purchase and install different apps for Windows 8.1 and for Windows Phone. This wasn't a problem with iOS and Android phones and tablets, which all shared the same OS, but it greatly annoyed many Windows users and developers who resented having to buy or create two apps instead of one.

That was back when Windows and Windows Phone were separate operating systems, but now Windows 10 will be the same OS across all devices, including Internet of Things (IoT) devices and the Xbox One.

This means that developers are already writing what Microsoft are calling *Universal Apps* for Windows 8.1 and Windows Phone 8.1, and these will also work on Windows 10.

There are a few changes coming to the way we interact with apps in Windows 10, however. I mentioned earlier in this chapter that the Charms menu from Windows 8 was gone, but you still need to be able to access functions like Search, Share, and Settings for individual apps. To get around this problem, the Charms have now moved within each app to a hamburger menu in the top left of the app (either windowed on the desktop or full-screen). Here you can access the Charms and also the (...) app commands menu (sometimes known as the app bar) (see Figure 2-13).

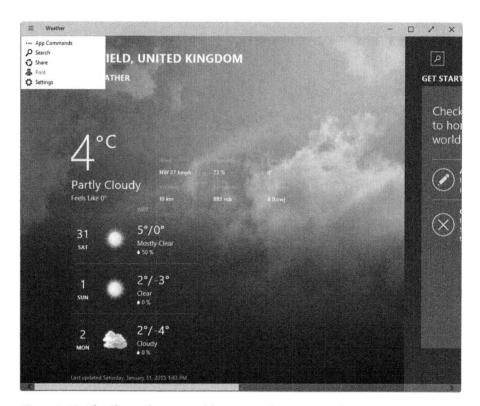

Figure 2-13. *The Charms have moved for Universal Apps in Windows 10*

In the top right of the app, nestled in with the minimize, maximize, and close buttons, is a new button that will toggle the app between full-screen and windowed modes. This is for those who wish to use Universal Apps on the desktop with a keyboard and mouse.

■ **Note**   It's been confirmed that some Universal Apps will come with a *Back* button in their top left corner. This will appear where it is appropriate within apps and will aid in moving to previous pages within the app.

Revamped Windows App Store

Microsoft has also revamped the Windows Store (see Figure 2-14) and has stated that for Windows 10 it will also include desktop programs and "other digital content," which might include music, video, and Xbox games.

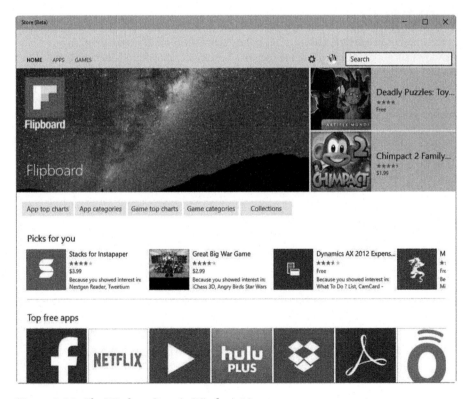

Figure 2-14. The Windows Store in Windows 10

What desktop software will appear in the Windows Store remains to be seen, as Microsoft charges a royalty for every app sold, and as such the large software houses like Adobe and Sony are unlikely to want part of their revenue taken by Microsoft.

■ **Note** Desktop software already features in the Windows Store in Windows 8.1, but only links to the developers' website are supported. Windows 10 will allow you to download and install desktop software directly from the store.

For smaller software houses, however, being able to include their desktop apps in the Windows Store will greatly aid discoverability, and it will help reassure Windows users that the software they are downloading is genuine and not loaded with malware.

Microsoft has also said that Windows Store functionality will be available for businesses through Microsoft Azure. Companies will be able to set up their own company stores that contain both bespoke apps and their choices of apps from the main Windows Store.

Summary

In this chapter I've detailed some of the major new features and changes coming to Windows 10, and I think you'll agree they're all pretty significant. In later chapters I'll look at many more features that are specific to desktop users, productivity, and businesses in more detail.

Before that, however, we'll look at what is happening to Windows 10 away from the PC—on smartphones, the Xbox One game console, IoT devices such as smart TVs, and more besides.

CHAPTER 3

■ ■ ■

Windows 10 for Phone and Other Devices

If you remember the days when you had a different operating system on every device, and when one didn't talk to any other, then you'll probably also remember how frustrating it could be. Whether you had to print out all your contacts and manually enter them into a new phone, or you did not have access to recent emails on a laptop because they'd already been downloaded using POP to your main PC, the "golden age" of computing could be a pain.

Fortunately, things are now very different, but perhaps not for the better. Technology has moved in a direction that some people feel has left us with fewer freedoms. Often I hear people talk of the tech company "lock-in." Whether this is with Apple, Google, or Microsoft, they all have operating systems and ecosystems of online services intended to get to you stay exclusively with them.

For many people the lock-in can be annoying, especially if you get bored of one smartphone system and fancy moving, for example, from Android to the new iPhone. Suddenly you have to buy all your apps again, and perhaps even abandon the online services you've been using.

I don't mind the lock in, for several reasons. Chief among these is that the integration between Microsoft's services has always been excellent, and the quality of those services is still higher on average than that of services offered by Google and Apple.

Take OneDrive and Office 365, for example. They're embedded deeply in all Microsoft products, and in addition to being useful services in their own right, they act as bridges between different Microsoft devices and platforms, such as PCs, tablets, and phones.

With Windows 10, Microsoft is taking this integration to the next level. They can do this because the same core operating system will be running on not just all of their own devices, such as PCs, tablets, phones, and the Xbox, but also extending outwards to Internet of Things (IoT) devices such as the Raspberry Pi.

In this chapter then, we'll look at the ecosystem outside of the PC to see where you will find Windows 10 and what its inclusion on different devices will mean for usability, accessibility, and productivity.

Windows 10 for Phone

I mentioned earlier that there were several reasons why I didn't mind the Microsoft lock-in, and Windows Phone is definitely up there as a top reason. I'm not an app guy and have always viewed Apple and Google's approach of filling the front screen of their devices with icons as just a way to push you into buying apps you don't need.

Google's widgets are a valuable step forward, but the Live Tiles we saw first with Windows Phone are just fantastic. Many of you will agree, I'm sure, that being able to check what that latest email or Facebook post is, or look at the current weather or news with just a glance is a great time (and battery) saver.

You'll be pleased to hear that Microsoft hasn't fiddled with any of this functionality in Windows 10 for Phone, and indeed they may still be expanding it.

You might have seen a (quickly withdrawn) video from Microsoft Research in the Far East in 2014 that showed Live Tiles that could be expanded into a full app, right on the Windows Start Screen. This enabled people to be able to open, for instance, a calculator quickly and without having to wait to load the app. I sincerely hope that Microsoft builds this functionality into Windows 10 and Windows 10 for Phone.

What Microsoft has done, however, is take all of the strengths of Windows Phone and expanded on them. You may already be familiar with some of this functionality if you've been using the latest Windows Phone 8.1 builds, which include Cortana. Cortana in Windows 10 for Phone works exactly as it does on the desktop, as I detailed in Chapter 2.

The Notification Center

Windows Phone 8.1 introduced us to a notification center on a Windows device for the first time. It was a central store for all messages and information from the OS, your email, messaging features, and installed apps. In addition, the Notification Center allowed you to pin a number of quick-action buttons to the top of your screen, such as Wi-Fi on/off and the Quiet Hours feature, which silences notifications and audio and can optionally send a text message to anyone who called or texted you to tell them you were busy.

Windows 10 for Phone expands notifications and the Notification Center in several ways. The first and perhaps the most prominent way is that you can now pin many more quick-action buttons to the top of the center (see Figure 3-1).

Figure 3-1. *You can pin more quick-action buttons to the Notification Center in* *Windows 10 for Phones*

Depending on the size of the screen on your existing Windows Phone, the number of pinable icons can be limited. On my own Lumia 1020 I can only have four, and would like extras.

You will only see the top row of buttons, perhaps your most commonly used ones, when opening the Notification Center, but an *expand/collapse* link to the bottom right of the icons will allow you to display all the pinned quick-action buttons.

This expand/collapse functionality has been included in other aspects of notifications too. All of the notifications that appear can be interacted with in several new ways, as follows.

- You can **expand** notifications to read more details about them, which is useful for a weather alert or email that is truncated by being limited to one line on your phone's screen.

- Some notifications will have **interaction** buttons that allow you to perform actions without having to first enter the app to do so, such as dismissing an alarm or replying to a text message. This functionality will require in-app support so it won't be universally available.

- Just as you could swipe a toast notification away in Windows 8 and 8.1, Windows 10 for Phone allows you to quickly **swipe right to clear a notification**. It's also expected that a two-finger swipe will let you clear all your notifications in one action.

Figure 3-2. *You can interact with toasts without having to open the app*

When toast notifications appear on your screen, perhaps to alert you to a new incoming message, email, or Facebook post, you can interact with these messages directly from within the toast. A good example of this is being able to read a text message in the toast and reply, there and then, without first having to enter the messaging app. Other toasts will include buttons and other controls that allow you to interact with the toast or dismiss it, such as with an alarm.

■ **Note** Another useful feature with notifications is that, should you turn your phone off, it'll give you an "*in case you forgot*" message with any upcoming appointments or reminders you have set.

Enhanced Keyboard

The on-screen keyboard in Windows 8.1 and Windows Phone has always had some extremely useful and often hidden functionality, such being able to tap and hold on a letter to display its foreign equivalents, including accented characters. However, the on-screen keyboard in Windows 10 has been greatly enhanced and expanded. For example, on desktop, laptop, and tablet PCs it now features predictive text, allowing you to create messages more quickly, as it intelligently predicts what word you're likely to type next.

The on-screen keyboard in Windows 10 for Phones has been enhanced in two significant ways. First, you can grab the keyboard and drag it to the left or right side of the screen. This will be useful for people using larger-screened phones or phablets.

Additionally, a new microphone icon is now displayed above the keyboard, allowing you to dictate what you want to write instead of typing it. Microsoft has made great strides with their voice recognition technology in recent years and has further refined its abilities in Windows 10 for Phone. For example, this new text-to-speech feature allows you to dictate into virtually any text field in the OS or app.

Enhancements to grammar and spelling algorithms now mean that your smartphone can fill in the correct grammar for your particular usage automatically and tell when you mean to use a particular homophone, such as saying "too" instead of "two."

Finally, and this will be great news to all fans of Lenovo's laptops, the Windows 10 for Phone keyboard includes a cursor "nipple" (see Figure 3-3).

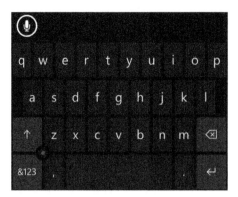

Figure 3-3. The phone keyboard now includes a Lenovo-style cursor nipple

One of the biggest criticisms with the Windows Phone keyboard has been the problems you face trying to change a specific character in the middle of a word, with the whole word often having to be retyped. This new nipple, which can be seen in the bottom left corner of the keyboard, now acts as a draggable cursor, enabling you to move in four directions to wherever you need to be in your text.

Customization

One of the biggest strengths of the Windows operating system, and a primary reason for its success over the last thirty years, is that it's always been the most configurable and customizable operating system available. No matter what it is you want to change in Windows, from skinning the OS to tweaking Registry keys, it has been possible to achieve, and entire third-party industries have grown up to support this.

Customization was very late to come to Windows Phone, however, and there were good reasons for it. A smartphone OS isn't the same as one on the desktop, where you can save Restore Points or a factory backup image, or just boot from a DVD and reinstall everything from scratch.

Smartphones have very limited storage and connection potential, but perhaps more critically, they tap directly into our bank accounts and other payment systems in a way our PCs likely never will. On your smartphone you can quickly run up enormous bills if you create an ecosystem in which malware can surreptitiously send text messages or trick you into making international phone calls. Consequently, permitting apps to change low-level OS settings and features on a smartphone can create a security risk far more easily, and possibly much more seriously, than on a desktop PC.

Inevitably however, customization options began to appear, and by the time of Windows 8.1 we had Live Tile backgrounds and new color schemes.

Windows 10 for Phones naturally expands this functionality, primarily providing the ability to at last set a full wallpaper for your Start screen. This sits in the background instead of inside the tiles (see Figure 3-4).

Figure 3-4. *You can set full-background wallpapers in Windows 10 for Phone*

Additionally, Tiles can now be transparent so that the wallpaper will partially show through. Should you prefer, on-Live Tile wallpaper options also exist that will place the wallpaper image on the Tiles themselves, rather than on the background.

None of this means we can change the typefaces or other advanced customization features of our handsets, but they're a very welcome step in the right direction.

Better Organized Settings

If you've used a Windows Phone up to this point then you'll know that the phone Settings were a jumbled mess. This wasn't helped by third-party companies such as Nokia being able to inject their own additional options in the main Settings menu. With Windows 10 for Phone this has been rationalized and brought in sync with the new Settings panel on PCs and tablets (see Figure 3-5).

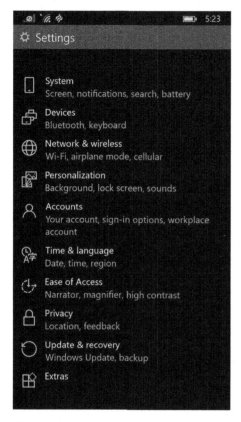

Figure 3-5. *Settings in Windows 10 for Phone are much improved*

The more complicated smartphone operating systems get, the more difficult it can be to find what you need. A new category-based approach helps you quickly find the settings on the phone that you're looking for. This new view helps rationalize the OS and generally improves the whole configuration experience.

Additional Improvements in Windows 10 for Phone

While not all of the final features and enhancements in Windows 10 for Phone have been revealed, there are already some compelling improvements and additions. I'll detail them here in no particular order, except for the one I feel is most welcome.

Like many smartphone users, I use the Alarms app a lot, almost every day, in fact, which must make it my most-used app after email, messaging, and Facebook. I was delighted to see that it's been enhanced in Windows 10 for Phone with the addition of a timer, stopwatch, and world clock (see Figure 3-6).

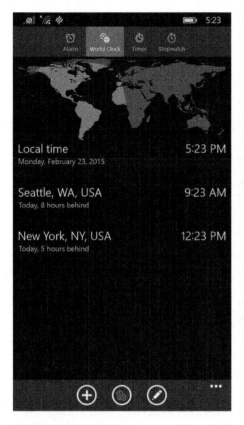

Figure 3-6. *The Alarms app now features timers and a world clock*

This world clock isn't like any basic world clock app either, as genuine thought has gone into its implementation. As well as being able to see what the time is in Seattle and New York (where Microsoft and my publishers can be found), you can now compare different times for different cities around the world. This might sound like only a moderately useful feature, but it's amazing how difficult the information can be to get when you *do* need it.

When Windows Phone first launched, we could store files on our phones and open them using the built-in Office and PDF apps. However, it took some time for an actual File Explorer app to be released by Microsoft, and then it was a downloadable extra.

Now, a full File Explorer has been included in Windows 10 for Phones, allowing us to better organize our collections of files, documents, music, videos, and photos (see Figure 3-7).

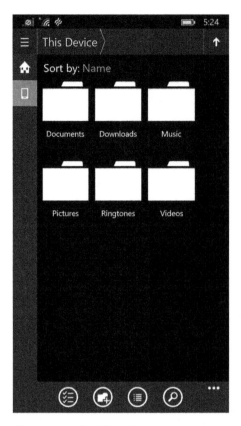

Figure 3-7. *The File Explorer app is now part of the OS*

The Calculator app has been enhanced with the tools we need while we're on the move, such as full scientific and programmer modes, and every form of conversion calculation you can think of, except for currencies (see Figure 3-8).

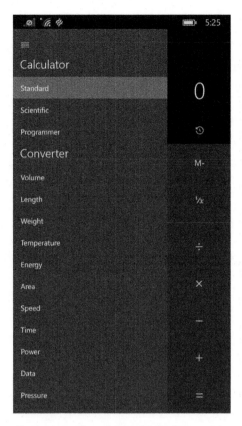

Figure 3-8. *The enhanced Calculator app*

There's also a new Sound Recorder app, which many will find useful for note-taking or in meetings and lectures.

Microsoft's headline app so far, however, is Photos. Just like its desktop cousin, it's been enhanced to automatically aggregate all the photos you have stored on your various Windows 10 devices and cloud services, such as OneDrive.

Also like the Windows 10 desktop app, photos can be grouped and displayed in different ways, such as by date, location, or the people included (see Figure 3-9).

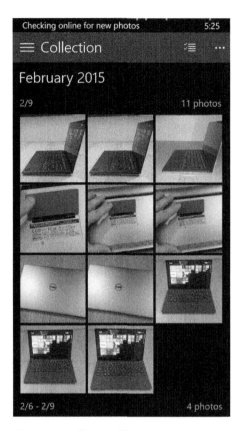

Figure 3-9. *The new Photos app*

These features are intelligent and, again like the desktop app, can help you find all your photos taken in a specific location, say, Austria, by using metadata such as date taken and geotagging. It can also use face recognition to find all the photos of your friend Phil.

So What's in It for Businesses?

All of the new and enhanced features in Windows 10 for Phone that I've detailed so far are aimed at making it easier to use and configure the OS for consumers, but businesses are certainly not left out. This is Windows 10, and that means, for the first time, every security and manageability feature that's available in the desktop version of the OS is also available here. There might not be a Group Policy app, but full management of Windows 10 phones is available in Windows Server.

Crucially, all of the new and enhanced security features in Windows 10 will be available on phones, and Bring Your Own Device (BYOD) manageability is included too. You can find out about all the new and enhanced business and security features available for businesses in Windows 10 when you read chapters 5 and 6.

Xbox One

When Microsoft said that Windows 10 would be "one OS for every device in your life," they weren't kidding. I'll talk later in this chapter about the Internet of Things, but one of the devices running Windows 10 that you're likely to have is an Xbox One games console.

It makes sense for Microsoft to port Windows 10 to the Xbox One console (it won't be ported to the Xbox 360), if only for reasons of security and manageability. It's much cheaper for any company to fix security and stability flaws on a single OS platform than across many, especially when they have so much in common to begin with.

We've not yet seen the new Xbox environment for Windows 10 in any detail, but everything you've read here about an integrated Settings environment and universal apps will apply. Universal apps are a good case in point, as they'll be able to run on your Xbox in the same way they run on your phone, PC, and tablet. This offers new opportunities for gaming in Windows 10. You might, for example, have a really great game on your Windows Phone that has you utterly hooked. If you're lucky it'll also be available for your desktop. With Universal Apps, it's almost certain that you'll be able to play the same game on your Xbox when you get home.

Integration doesn't stop there, however. The new Xbox Live apps for your desktop, tablet, and phone will allow you to manage your player profile, achievements, and more from those devices (see Figure 3-10).

Figure 3-10. *Xbox One will run Windows 10*

Perhaps the coolest feature will be that you can stream Xbox One games from the console to any Windows 10 PC or tablet, meaning you can continue to play your games when the TV is in use for "Better Call Saul" or "Game of Thrones."

Another major benefit of having Windows 10 running on the Xbox One is that you will be able to play games online with people who are using a Windows 10 PC, laptop, or tablet. Not all players will need an Xbox One console to participate. All you will need is the game available for the different devices.

The inclusion of Microsoft's new graphics rendering engine, DirectX 12, will result in ever-more realistic and smooth gameplay, and Windows 10 will allow you to capture image and video clips of your gaming in real time as you play and share them with online communities.

It's probably in gaming that Windows 10 sees some of its greatest potential, especially with Internet of Things devices, which I'll talk about shortly. Gaming has always been incredibly popular on Windows PCs, and Windows 10 looks certain to take this popularity to the next level.

The Internet of Things

First, I should explain what the Internet of Things (IoT) is, as you may have heard of it but not be completely familiar with the concept. Basically, the Internet of Things is an idea whereby all of our home and work devices and appliances are connected to the Internet and have improved functionality as a result.

Some of this has already appeared, with solar power systems able to communicate with you remotely via an app, a refrigerator able to do whatever it is an Internet fridge might need to do (even I get confused by that one), a microwave or oven that can download recipes and cooking times, or a bathroom mirror that can display your day's appointments.

IoT devices even extend outside of the home; cars can be Internet-connected to read us emails as they arrive, display appointment details, provide live route-planning, and to allow us to make a quick video call over Skype.

Some IoT devices have existed in the workplace for a while, such as photocopiers and printers that can send emails and save documents to cloud backup services. The Microsoft Surface Hub, which I detail in Chapter 5, is an IoT PC.

Lastly, if you're using an Internet-connected smart TV, you are using an IoT device. They are quite literally everywhere!

Microsoft is determined that many more IoT devices will run Windows 10 in years to come, but how will this benefit us, if at all?

For myself, I rather like the idea of the bathroom mirror or refrigerator informing me of upcoming appointments or newly-arrived emails while I'm half-asleep early in the morning. I think that a touch-screen desk that instantly has access to my OneDrive would be extremely useful, especially when I need to quickly pull up an important file, and I believe the educational possibilities of IoT devices running Windows 10 are not to be underestimated.

Raspberry Pi 2

This brings me rather neatly to the subject of the Raspberry Pi (see Figure 3-11). For those of you who are unfamiliar with it, this is an inexpensive, bare-bones PC that was designed to help students learn how to write computer code.

Figure 3-11. *The Raspberry Pi 2 runs Windows 10*

The first Raspberry Pi was released to great fanfare in 2012. It featured a low-cost ARM processor, 256MB of memory, and storage only available through the addition of an SD memory card.

As an educational tool, the Raspberry Pi is highly effective, as it is able to run a wide range of operating systems and support many programming languages. It could connect to USB devices, a keyboard, mouse, and monitor, and even to the Internet.

This year the improved Raspberry Pi 2 was launched, and the enormous developer community for the platform simply demanded support for Windows. Microsoft was all too happy to oblige, and they announced at the beginning of February 2015 not only that Windows 10 would run on the Raspberry Pi 2, but also that the OS would be completely free to the development community through the Windows Developer Program for IoT. The version of Windows available for the Raspberry Pi 2 will likely be very similar to the 8-inch or smaller devices edition. This means there will be no desktop version, for reasons of licensing.

Being able to purchase a small PC for just $35 and write and run Windows 10 apps on it will be a hugely exciting prospect for the developer and educational communities alike, and it's definitely something to look forward to.

Summary

One operating system, for every device in your life, was what Microsoft said when they first announced Windows 10 to the world, and 2015 is, quite frankly, only the start of it. PCs, laptops, Ultrabooks, tablets, the Xbox One, phones, and the Raspberry Pi 2 are where things will begin, but let's not forget what's already been announced, such as the HoloLens, which I will talk about in Chapter 4, and the Surface Hub.

The potential of Windows 10 to be a global OS platform doesn't stop there, however. Your home automation or heating system could soon be powered by Windows 10, as might your car or even the kettle. The possibilities only end at the limits of the imagination of software and device developers.

So far in this book I've detailed the new and cool features in the Windows 10 OS, but that's only half the story. In the next chapter we'll begin to look at how this all fits together into a cohesive and more productive experience for users and businesses alike. Now, where's my phone? I need to tell the kettle to be boiled for when I get home.

CHAPTER 4

■ ■ ■

What's New for End Users?

So far in this book I've shown you the new headline features in Windows 10, including the Cortana personal assistant and various features coming to Windows 10 smartphones. The question remains, however: What will Windows 10 actually be like to use on your PC?

Microsoft has made quite a bit of noise about their productivity focus for this new operating system, and I've mentioned it in these pages on more than one occasion.

Whether you're using your PC at home or at work, you don't want to be hamstrung by an interface that's difficult to use or OS features that aren't discoverable or intuitive. In this chapter, I'll guide you through what's new and improved on the Windows desktop and show you how it'll make a positive impact on your PC use.

Multiple Desktops

Unless you're using a small Windows tablet or you just use Windows on a phone, you'll spend much, if not all, of your time on the desktop. When you start Windows 10, all appears much as before, with the Taskbar along the bottom of your screen, a Windows key in the bottom left, and the system tray and clock in the bottom right.

Don't be fooled though, as major and significant changes have been made to the desktop in Windows 10. Each change is either a refinement of an existing feature or something new entirely.

The ability to have multiple desktops on a PC has been a feature of GNU/Linux for years, and many plug-ins have existed for Windows to allow you to add the feature. Windows 10, however, is the first time Microsoft has natively included this much-requested feature in the OS. It's run from an icon on the Taskbar, and you can identify it by two rectangular blocks, one in front of the other (see Figure 4-1).

Figure 4-1. *You can launch multiple desktops from the Taskbar*

Clicking this icon will display all your open windows as thumbnails while also displaying a dark bar across the bottom of your screen with an *Add a desktop* button in its center (see Figure 4-2).

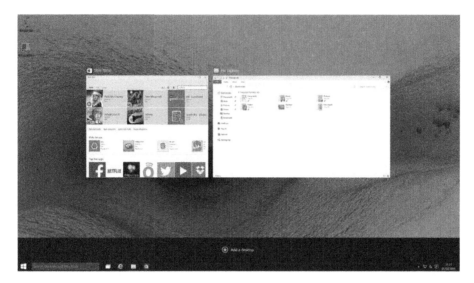

Figure 4-2. *The Add a desktop button is bottom center on the screen*

When you have multiple desktops open, they will appear as small, live thumbnails on this dark bar (see Figure 4-3).

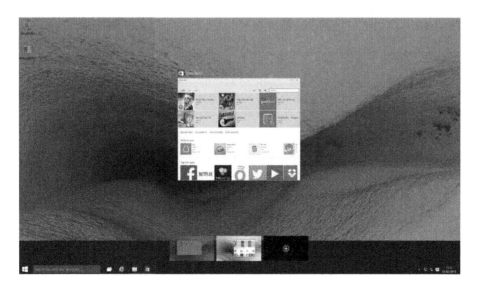

Figure 4-3. *It's simple to manage multiple desktops in Windows 10*

The methods for moving apps between desktops hadn't been finalized in Windows 10 by the time I wrote this, but right-clicking (touching and holding) an app thumbnail will display an options menu, in which a move option is available. It will be possible in the final release of Windows 10 to use a keyboard combination shortcut to move apps to different desktops, and it's also expected that you'll be able to drag and drop apps to different desktops.

You can close an entire desktop by clicking the Close icon on its thumbnail, which appears when you mouse over the icon. The touch method for closing a desktop has not yet been finalized. Closing a desktop doesn't mean any apps open on that desktop will also be closed. When you close a desktop, any open apps are automatically moved to the nearest open desktop.

Multiple desktops can be extremely useful, especially in the business space. For example, when working in my home office I will have Internet Explorer and Outlook open on one desktop, Microsoft Word for writing on a second, and perhaps a couple of virtual machines for testing as well as screenshots open on a third.

Alternatively, you could have your work apps open on one desktop, and Amazon and Minesweeper open on another (though when the time comes for a meeting with your employer about this, you didn't get the idea from me).

The Return of the Start Menu

One of the largest criticisms of Windows 8 was the removal of the Start Menu from the desktop, and its replacement with the full-screen *Start Screen* and the All Apps View.

When the Start Menu was first introduced in Windows 95 (yes it really is that old), it received instant praise, and when it was refined further in Windows Vista and Windows 7 so that huge fly-out menus didn't appear from the All Programs link, it became universally popular. Well, you'll be delighted to hear that the Start Menu is making a triumphant return in Windows 10 and has been refined yet again (see Figure 4-4).

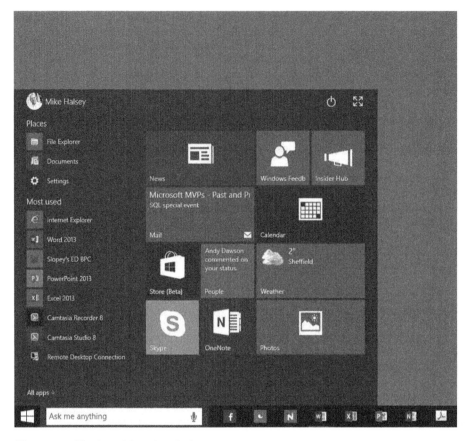

Figure 4-4. The Start Menu in Windows 10

I've got to be honest—I never personally liked the Start Menu after Windows 7 was released, as in many ways pinning app icons to the Taskbar and launching files from their jumplists is a significantly faster way to launch any app in Windows.

I've also harangued Windows program managers over the years to include the ability to create Taskbar program groups, where you can drag one app icon onto another to create a pop-up apps group. They told me they'd considered it, but they haven't implemented it yet.

So what's new with this changed Start Menu, and are the changes an improvement? The first thing you'll notice is that tiles for Universal Apps are now pinnable to its right side. These are completely optional, and if you want to use the Start Menu with just your desktop programs and no pinned Live Tiles, you can do just that.

Should you want some Live Tiles, however—and I'll detail in a minute a good reason why you might—they can be resized in the same way as on the Windows 8.1 Start Screen and dragged around to rearrange them, even into different tile groups.

Live Tiles can be generally useful because of the information they provide. In addition, being able to press the Windows key and, at a glance, see the headers for your latest received emails as well as the news headlines and weather can not only help keep you more informed, but can also boost your productivity since you might need to open those apps or news websites often.

On the Windows 7 Start Menu, options for various PC locations, such as your documents and computer File Explorer views, the Control Panel, and Devices and Printers, were found in the right panel. These have now been moved to the top left of the Start Menu in a *Places* section.

Beneath this is the list of your *Most Used* apps and then finally any *Recently Installed* apps will appear. The *All Apps* button sits in the bottom left of the Start Menu and presents a list of all the apps installed on your PC in a way that will be instantly familiar to users of Windows 7.

In the final release of Windows 10 these views will be highly configurable, just as they were in Windows 7, with apps viewable in a variety of different ways. You can also drag Universal Apps directly out of the All Apps list into the tiled area on the right of Start Menu.

■ **Note**   It's expected, but has not been confirmed, that in the final release of Windows 10 you will be able to drag Universal App tiles onto the desktop, where they can be pinned and used as live information widgets.

There are three more buttons at the top of the Start Menu. In the top left is your user picture, which you can click for options to change your user account settings, log out, or lock the PC. At the top right of the Start Menu are a power button—with Sleep, Shut down, and Restart options—and a maximize button, which will toggle the Start Menu between a full-screen mode and a windows mode.

In an early build of Windows 10 the edges of the Start Menu could be grabbed with a mouse and dragged around to resize it. This is useful if you have a lot of tiles pinned to the Start Menu, but the feature was removed for the builds used to write this book. Hopefully this feature will see a return for the final release of the OS.

Improved App Switching with Task View

It might seem obvious to us now, but switching between running apps in Windows versions before Windows 10 was often hindered by the small thumbnail sizes of the apps. The Flip 3D view of Vista provided large thumbnails, but wasn't very popular with users, and so Windows 7 reverted to just the standard Alt-Tab way of switching between open apps.

Windows 10 does make this app switching easier, however, simply by making the thumbnails larger (see Figure 4-5). They're also live, so you can see exactly what's going on in the apps at that time.

Figure 4-5. *Improved app switching in Windows 10*

You'll also see in the figure that the apps are appropriately and fully labeled, making it easier to identify what's what. I don't know about you, but if you've had multiple File Explorer windows open, switching between them and finding the right one in the past has been a hit and miss affair.

Task View can also be controlled with gestures from your laptop's trackpad, and I'll detail how to do so later in this chapter.

Four-Way Snap!

I don't know about you, but I loved the desktop Snap feature when it was introduced in Windows 7. Being able to quickly snap two windows to the left and right side of the screen so I could transfer files or compare two web pages or documents, and then snap them away and have them revert to their original size, was hugely useful.

I always felt it limiting, however, that this only worked with two windows. I often have to simultaneously shuffle video and other files between different drives on my PC as well as network storage locations. Well, the good news is that Snap has been improved in Windows 10 so that it now supports four-way snap (see Figure 4-6).

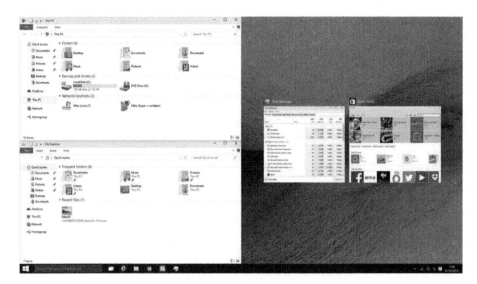

Figure 4-6. Windows 10 supports four-way snap

You can still drag apps to the far left and right of your screen to use snap in the two-way split-screen view as before. In addition, you can drag apps to the four corners of your screen to snap them top left, top right, bottom left, and bottom right.

When you snap a window in Windows 10, the remaining space will show thumbnail images for your remaining open apps. If you click one of these it will automatically fill the remaining space in a two-, three-, or four-way split view. Alternatively, you can click one of the apps that's already snapped, or the desktop, to return there.

Search from the Taskbar

In Chapter 2 I spoke about Cortana's inclusion in Windows 10 and of the productivity benefits it can bring. Not all countries will benefit from Cortana when Windows 10 launches, however, and some users will see a search icon instead.

Regardless of whether or not you use Cortana in Windows 10, you can change the Taskbar icon to a search box by right-clicking it and choosing the appropriate option, enabling you to search both your PC and the Internet directly from the Taskbar (see Figure 4-7).

Figure 4-7. You can search directly from the Taskbar

Searching from this box works in exactly the same way as I detailed in Chapter 2, and it can save valuable time since you don't have to open a web browser to navigate to Bing, Google, or another search engine.

■ **Note**   For people using Windows 10 on a touch device, such as a tablet, the desktop on-screen keyboard now supports full autocorrect and predictive text. These have been features in Windows Phone for a while, and it's great to see them used throughout Windows 10.

Improved File Explorer

It should be noted that File Explorer in Windows 10 is going through something of an upheaval, and so the version seen in the Technical Preview is far from the finished product.

One interesting addition, however, is that by default (though you can change this) the main view when you open a File Explorer window is the new *Quick Access* pane (see Figure 4-8).

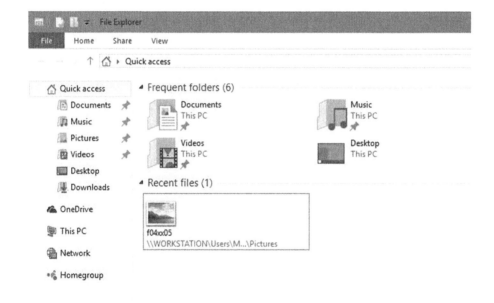

Figure 4-8. *File Explorer now opens into a Quick Access section*

This new view will show you the most recently utilized folders, disk locations, and files, enabling you to quickly gain access to the documents, files, and locations you are currently working with.

Anything can be pinned to the Quick Access view, which replaces the Favorites pane from Windows 7 and Windows 8.1. This includes folders, local and network drives, and files. Pinning an item to the Quick Access section doesn't just display it in the tree view on the left side of File Explorer windows, but also in the main view.

Otherwise, File Explorer is currently unchanged, though we can expect refinements to include better touch support, likely with Ribbon UI enhancements that space out buttons and options for when Tablet mode is activated on the PC.

Touch and Trackpad Gestures

Whether you will use Windows 10 with a touchscreen or on a laptop, you'll be using touch, and in this new OS the ways in which you can interact with the OS are benefitting from welcome improvements. Not all the gestures for Windows 10 have been finalized, but Microsoft is expected to further refine the touch gestures and controls for the OS.

Additionally new trackpad gestures will be available to laptop users. These include but are not limited to the following:

You can **Show [the] Desktop** with a three-finger swipe downwards on the trackpad. This gesture will automatically minimize all the windows on your screen (useful, perhaps, if the boss walks past while you're shopping on Amazon).

You can also reverse this (after the boss is out of view) by swiping upwards with three fingers on your trackpad to **Restore [all] Windows** on the desktop to their previous locations.

To open **Task View** in Windows 10 and see large thumbnail windows of all your running apps, swipe upwards with three fingers on the trackpad, the same gesture used to restore all your minimized windows.

Once in the Task View you can swipe left and right on the trackpad to move through the available apps, keeping your fingers on the trackpad while you do this. To select an app, lift your finger off the trackpad.

Overall, gestures such as multi-touch pinch-zoom controls are being improved upon for both touch and trackpad use, and we can expect to see additional gestures announced by Microsoft nearer the final release of Windows 10.

Single Sign-On

One of the improvements Microsoft made to Windows 8.1 and Windows Phone 8.1 was the ability to automatically sync your website usernames and passwords between various PCs using a Microsoft Account.

With Windows 10 they want to extend this functionality further by providing new single-sign-on (SSO) extensions. Full details of this are sketchy, but the aim is to make it simpler to log into multiple services that require the same username and password.

This will certainly work with a Microsoft Account and Windows Domain services, such as Azure and Active Directory. It remains to be seen if the functionality will also include other companies that provide multiple services, such as Google and Apple.

The final aim of SSO is that you will only be prompted for your username and/or password when security is crucial, for example when changing your account and billing settings with Microsoft.

OneDrive and OneDrive for Business

Microsoft is fully behind its cloud services strategy, and products including OneDrive and Office 365 are crucial to the company's prosperity going forward.

In recent years the company has made great improvements to its OneDrive cloud sync and backup service. These have included expanding the storage available to consumers and businesses, improving maximum file size limits, and so on.

One of the best, and most envied, OneDrive features in Windows 8.1 was its use of file placeholders. You could have tens or even hundreds of gigabytes of files stored in your OneDrive account. On a desktop PC with a large hard disk it wouldn't be a problem to also keep a local copy of these files, but on a tablet or Ultrabook, which typically come with very small amounts of storage, you could also keep all your files and access them whenever you needed. Windows 8.1 did this by using placeholders instead of the actual file. These placeholders would look like the file, report the correct size of the file, and so on, but instead they'd just be shortcut links to the actual file that was stored in your OneDrive account.

When you opened a placeholder, assuming you had a live Internet connection, the actual file would be downloaded and then stored and synced locally from the PC until such time as you right-clicked on it and told Windows to only make it available offline again. This was a tremendously clever idea, and it's being further refined in Windows 10 with the addition of support for Microsoft's OneDrive for Business service.

Previously, to use OneDrive for Business you needed to download a separate sync engine, which has remained separate until now. Windows 10 will unify them into a single sync engine so both can be managed quickly and simply from within Windows 10 itself.

The full ramifications of this aren't yet clear, though it's unlikely you'll be able to combine the two services into one large storage pool. OneDrive for Business is not without its flaws, however, a major flaw being that after a reinstall or reimage of the PC you have to resync the entire file library to your PC again, which is not something that the consumer version of OneDrive suffers from.

Hopefully OneDrive will take on new functionality, and the current limits of the OneDrive for Business sync engine will be eradicated in the final release of Windows 10.

Gaming and Xbox Streaming

Gaming has always been extremely important to the PC, and recent research has showed that game-development companies still place the PC at the top of their priority list, ahead of consoles such as the Xbox One and Playstation 4. This is despite the apparent focus placed on smartphone gaming.

With Windows 8, Microsoft introduced new Xbox features, though these were limited to a couple of apps and some games that could synchronize achievements with your Xbox Live account.

Windows 10 will take gaming to the next level with a new graphics rendering engine, DirectX 12, partnering with a truly cross-device operation (see Figure 4-9).

Figure 4-9. *Cross-device gaming is improved in Windows 10*

New features include the ability to play the same game with a friend simultaneously on desktop, tablet, and/or the Xbox One console. By far the standout feature for gaming in Windows 10, however, is the ability to livestream gameplay from your Xbox console to a tablet or PC running Windows 10. This will allow you to play your Xbox One games on almost any Windows 10 device, and because the graphics are streamed, the device you're playing the game on doesn't need a lot of graphics power of its own. This streaming is achieved over your home Wi-Fi network and will enable you to use a new generation of Xbox One controllers with multiple PC devices.

New Apps Coming to Windows 10

As you might expect, the launch of a new operating system will also include a refresh for the Universal Apps bundled with and available for your PC. Generally, updates will be available for all the main apps, including Mail (which will become Outlook), People, Calendar, Photos, Videos, Music, and more.

Microsoft hasn't said much about what new functionality these new apps will bring or how they may tie into the new store that Microsoft has said will include "other types of digital content" alongside apps and games.

One app they have spoken about, however, is the new Photos app, which includes two very interesting new features. The first of these is auto-enhance mode, which will apply simple and non-destructive enhancements to your photos to improve skin tone, color balance, contrast, or brightness.

A new albums feature will automatically aggregate the photos you have stored on your PC(s), phone, and OneDrive account into a single hub where they will be automatically sorted and categorized depending on the people in them, the location they were taken at, and so on.

This is a feature have I used extensively myself over the years by manually tagging photos in a custom pictures library in File Explorer. Windows 10 doing this on its own and letting me search automatically for photos taken in Germany or featuring my friend Larry will make organizing and searching our ever-expanding photo libraries much simpler.

Microsoft HoloLens

Microsoft's major Windows 10 announcements in January 2015 were completely overshadowed by the unveiling of the HoloLens headset at the end of the event.

The HoloLens, a prototype of which can be seen in Figure 4-10, is a natural and logical extension to the Kinect sensor and several other Microsoft prototype technologies that would have allowed us to interact with the world around us in different ways.

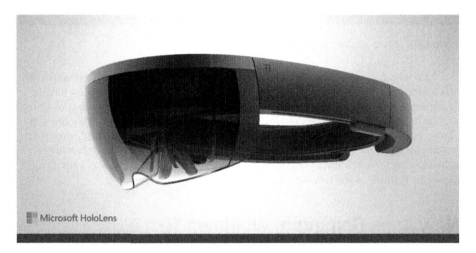

Figure 4-10. *The HoloLens headset*

The aim of HoloLens is two-fold. First, as seen in Figure 4-11, the headset will enable the overlaying of virtual objects in the real world, such as playing a large video on the wall of your living room, or placing a social media readout on your refrigerator door.

Figure 4-11. *Interacting with the world around you with HoloLens*

Second, the headset will allow you to interact with your physical environment and other people in new ways, such as chasing monsters around your own living room, creating a virtual Minecraft castle on a table, or building a 3D model for printing in thin air.

Additionally, the demos for HoloLens showed people working on Windows 10 tablets while being able to see what the wearer of the headset was seeing, and then annotating objects in that view with instructions, such as which pipe to unscrew or where in the engine they could find the manifold.

As you move your head in this virtual world the overlaid objects remain static, giving them a sense of real substance, and each can be interacted with using hand and finger gestures (though not actually touched or grabbed... yet!).

Reviewers who've had a chance to use HoloLens have described it as extremely realistic and even "magical," with the virtual objects not appearing as though they're on a screen, less than one inch from your eyes, but instead projected directly onto a real object across the room.

HoloLens will be out in the "Windows 10 timeframe," according to Microsoft, which puts it sometime in the next couple of years. Pricing has not been announced, and the success of the product will sit entirely with the quality and available of apps.

As a media or educational device, however, the HoloLens shows great potential, and I personally can't wait to try one for myself.

Summary

It's clear that the new and updated features in Windows 10 just keep coming, and the focus Microsoft has placed on helping us all to achieve more, faster and more effectively than we have before, be that at home, college, or at work, is obvious.

The workplace is a hugely important part of Microsoft's business, and all the user interface improvements in the world won't be enough to convince companies to upgrade. With this in mind, I'll detail in the next chapter what Microsoft is doing for business, with productivity, deployment, security, and apps, to help them get more from their PCs while creating the stability, scalability, and robustness that they demand.

■ ■ ■

CHAPTER 5

What's New for Businesses?

When it was launched, Windows 8 was very much focused on what Microsoft saw at the time as being the future of modern computing: tablets and touch screens. As such, it was perceived that this was entirely a consumer release and the OS had nothing to offer businesses. This actually is not true, and if you haven't used Windows 8 and Windows 8.1 before, it's worth beginning this chapter by introducing new features to you that have now been around for a while and that you'll also get in Windows 10.

Business Features in Windows 8

We live in a world now where people are increasingly using, or wanting to use, their own PCs and devices in the workplace. This might be somebody wanting to use their own laptop (because it's newer and more powerful than the one work provided), someone wanting to use their own phone to avoid having two handsets, or an executive gushing over the iPad they got for their birthday.

BYOD, officially known as Bring Your Own Device, though often referred to as Bring Your Own Disaster, presents unique challenges for system administrators. Not the least of these challenges is that because they don't own the device, they don't have full control over its security, updates, and compatibility.

Windows 8 introduced new management features that worked with Windows Server 2012. Chief among these was **Workplace Join**. Traditionally, you'd connect a laptop or other mobile device to a company server system using a Virtual Private Network (VPN). Workplace Join was designed to allow BYOD PCs to connect, and it offered some additional functionality over a straight VPN connection.

The most important functionality of Workplace Join was that companies could specify that BYOD PCs and mobile devices had to permit a certain level of remote administration. This included barring the machine if it didn't meet a required minimum level of security, and permitted the company to remotely wipe all the data and files relevant to the business whenever they chose.

Windows Server 2012 also brought management support for non-Microsoft devices, such as those running iOS or Android, and any device running the Open Mobile Device Management (OMA-DM) specification could be easily managed in the same way as Windows 8 devices, without the need for third-party software.

Work Folders allowed the PC user access to files and documents on the network, but system administrators could specify what parts of the network could be accessed once a device was registered, thereby limiting the surface for malware and hacking attack.

For those people who wanted to use their work PC at home or in remote locations, but for whom a work laptop wasn't appropriate, **Windows To Go** could create a copy of their entire Windows installation, including installed apps and win32 desktop software, on a USB Flash Drive. This drive could be used on any PC capable of booting from USB and provided an additional level of security in that it prevented the user from seeing the hard disks of the host machine. This feature also helped protect the Windows To Go drive from malware infection.

Encryption was beefed up in Windows 8.1, with all new portable PCs (laptops and tablets) being required to offer a TPM chip and Bitlocker encryption by default. Additionally, biometric security was baked into the OS, with fingerprint login added to the impressive list (password, PIN, smartcard, picture password) of access methods for a device.

Other features useful to businesses included **Wi-Fi Direct** and **NFC,** allowing direct pairing of a PC with a compatible printer; **Miracast** for connecting to remote projectors and displays without the need for cables; and **Mobile Tethering,** so a PC with a 3G or 4G connection could share this with up to ten other devices.

Multi-Monitor improvements included the ability to independently scale individual displays, **PowerShell 4** brought new administration options for business, and **InstantGo** allowed people with compatible PCs to be up and running much more quickly than with older hardware.

All of these features are included in Windows 10 as well, so if you're still using Windows 7 or even XP in your business, you have a lot to look forward to before we even get to the extra features Windows 10 will introduce.

Universal Apps and Enterprise App Stores

When Microsoft first introduced their Metro/Modern/Universal App model (delete as applicable) it was widely derided by people in the business space as being for lightweight apps and consumers only.

I've always argued against this, for several reasons. First, working in education I experience first-hand the amount of data replication that we can find in the workplace. The Universal App *sharing* feature is useful for far more than sharing a photo from your Camera app with Facebook; it can also propagate data automatically from one app to several others, according to pre-programmed criteria.

Yes, the first Modern apps Microsoft released with Windows 8 were awful; there's no shame in admitting this. Some apps quickly rose to the top, however, including the excellent EMR Surface (see Figure 5-1), which cost $500 and helped clinicians manage their documentation process.

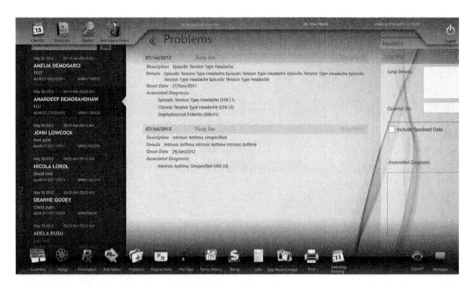

Figure 5-1. *The EMR Surface app for Windows 8*

EMR Surface and other high-end business apps proved that you can create extremely powerful business apps for Windows and that you don't lose any pixels on your screen by doing so.

With the advent of the Universal App, able to run across all Windows 10 devices from the phone and tablet to the desktop and even the huge Surface Hub with its 84-inch screen, new opportunities were created for businesses, many of whom are still running bespoke legacy software that was originally written for Windows XP (or perhaps even an earlier version of the OS).

A legitimate criticism of apps in Windows 8 was the available options for user-interface features. I was one of the many asking why an API for Microsoft's Ribbon interface wasn't included. The newly released beta versions of Word, Excel, and PowerPoint apps for Windows 10 include Ribbon functionality (see Figure 5-2), and we can expect this to be available within other apps too. The extra functionality accessible using the Ribbon interface is quite considerable.

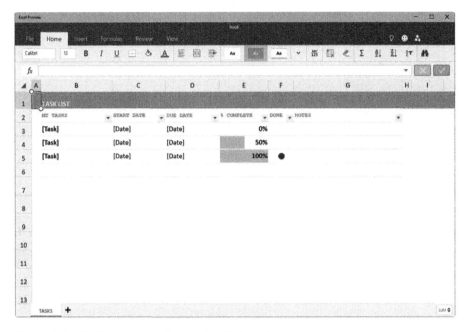

Figure 5-2. *The Ribbon comes to apps in Windows 10*

In addition to Universal Apps, Windows 10 introduces the facility for businesses to set up their own app stores using Microsoft Azure. Here you can provide your own business apps for Windows along with your selection of third-party apps and utilities. The feature is simple to set up and deploy across all Windows 10 devices.

Whatever device is in use then, be it a laptop, tablet, or phone, the same app with the same functionality will be available to the user. This ability to bring full desktop functionality to smaller devices will allow people to keep working, and being productive, when on the move and away from the office.

Managing Updates and Upgrades in the Workplace

Windows 10 will be the last major version of Windows. However, this doesn't mean that in three years' time Microsoft is dropping the product. Rather, it means that they're moving to the model adopted by Apple with OS X, in that the core OS will receive more regular and more minor updates.

Why are they doing this? In the case of Windows 10, a number of contributory factors come into play. It's become obvious in the years since Windows 8 was first unveiled that the desktop is going nowhere for business users. Despite the popularity of tablets and other touch-based PCs, Windows users worldwide made it abundantly clear that they want the desktop, and that they don't want the desktop to change.

Conversely, however, the touch interface Microsoft introduced with Windows Phone has been extremely successful, both on smartphones and also on tablets.

If you couple these reasons with Microsoft's strategy to, quite sensibly, use a single OS across a multitude of devices, from smartphones and PCs to the Xbox, IoT devices, and the HoloLens headset, it then makes sense to lock down a *final* version of the OS. These separate devices won't all follow a three-year upgrade cycle, Xbox being a great example. Windows is also extremely mature as a product, and it is a good time to lock it down.

Microsoft's intention then is to roll out annual free updates to the OS that include new and modified features and functionality. This might come as alarming news to some Enterprise users, though, who change their OS only every six or seven years, and then only after extensive testing has taken place to ensure all their hardware and software will work with it.

The good news here is that Microsoft has thought of that. Microsoft is splitting the updates and upgrades to Windows into two branches, one of which will be optional for Enterprise users.

Windows Update will continue to deliver security and stability fixes and patches for the OS, while a separate **Current branch for Business** will provide core OS updates to the Enterprise in a way that permits them to extensively test for compatibility before deploying.

Critical and important Windows Updates will continue to be subject to the same forced installation rules as with Windows 8.1, in that after a period of time they'll be installed automatically. The new business branch, however, won't be subject to these rules; instead the branch will go as long as three years before installation becomes necessary.

Simplifying Deployment

Deploying a new version of Windows across a business is a time-consuming and tricky process. It can take the best part of a couple of years to upgrade a large enterprise, and many months for even a small company.

With Windows 10, Microsoft is improving the deployment process by making it possible to upgrade the existing OS in-place, instead of using the wipe-and-load approach commonly used in the workplace.

One of the challenges with Windows 8 was upgrading the OS in-place. Only when upgrading from Windows 7 could you keep all of your files, settings, *and* installed win32 desktop software, but with Windows 8.1 and further kernel changes, this shifted again, permitting only files to be kept in some scenarios.

Microsoft has worked to improve the in-place upgrade experience in Windows 10, and they promise that all Windows 7, Windows 8, Windows 8.1, and Windows RT PCs on which an in-place upgrade is performed will be able to keep all files, settings, *and* both store and win32 apps during the process.

They've worked hard to maintain compatibility with older software and hardware, and indeed the hardware driver model is unchanged from Windows 7, so any PCs and hardware you're already using will work fine in Windows 10.

Windows 10's new configuration tools for Enterprise are also being improved, permitting much quicker configuration and provisioning of Wi-Fi, VPNs and email profiles, apps, language packs, security updates and certificates, and security policies. All of this will be done through remote management facilities, such as the Assessment and Deployment Toolkit (ADK), Microsoft Deployment Toolkit (MDK), and System Center Configuration Manager.

Azure and Active Directory Single Sign-on

There are many reasons why Windows 8 was resisted in the workplace, not the least of which is that most businesses were only just migrating to Windows 7 when Windows 8 was released. One of the coolest features in Windows 8, however, was also one of the most contentious, this being signing into the PC with a Microsoft Account.

Using this MS Account sign-on permitted synchronization of settings across different PCs; the use of the OneDrive cloud backup and sync service; and, crucially, access to the Windows store for apps.

Anybody who wanted to log in to a Windows 8 PC using a local account or a Domain didn't get these benefits. Now, for those people in business using Domains, this likely wouldn't have been an issue, unless they really needed to use Store apps, but with Microsoft creating new Enterprise app stores in Windows 10, the situation clearly needed to be improved.

Windows 10 will allow business users to use a single-sign-on (SSO) system with an Azure or Active Directory account to log in to the PC, the store, and more besides. This is all part of Microsoft taking a more connected approach to Windows 10 in the business space.

The Internet Explorer Question

Earlier in this book I talked about Microsoft's new web browser, codename Spartan, and how it is replacing Internet Explorer in Windows 10. Woah! Thought I heard you cry. Many businesses both need and rely on Internet Explorer for plug-in and intranet compatibility, so if it's removed, what the hell are you all to do?

Well, there's no need to panic, because Internet Explorer isn't going away. While Microsoft has not yet announced what versions of Windows will include IE, it's very likely that both the Professional and Enterprise editions of Windows 10 will still include Internet Explorer 11 (the version that shipped with Windows 8).

IE will still be able to be set as the default browser for the PC, and will be unchanged from the current Windows 8.1 version (though we may yet see new features aimed at maintaining compatibility for business users).

Identity Protection, Access Control, and VPN Updates

I'll focus on security in Windows 10 in much more depth in Chapter 6, but Windows 10 includes some valuable new security technologies. Chief among these are Identity Protection and Access Control. The former is a new system that uses Hyper-V virtualization technology to store identity and access tokens in a secure store where they can't be accessed by an attacker.

Access Control will employ a series of measures to restrict access to a specific PC to all but an authorized user. This will include improved biometric controls, some of which are already included in Windows 8.1, and new baked-in, two-factor authentication.

This latter system will use biometric sensors, or even the proximity of a Windows 10 Phone, to keep data and files on a PC safe and secure.

Virtual Private Networks (VPN) also include new security controls, including monitoring which apps can access data across the company network and permitting the restriction of specific communication ports and IP addresses.

Threat Resistance

Windows 10 will also provide the ability for companies to lock down devices so as to provide better resistance to malware and attacks. This works in several ways, including by only allowing trusted and digitally signed apps to run on the PC.

Businesses will be able to choose for themselves which apps are to be considered trustworthy, including both win32 and Universal apps.

BYOD Improvements in Windows 10

Bring Your Own Device (BYOD) management is already strong in Windows 8.1 and Windows Server 2012, and it's unclear what new features Microsoft will be bringing to the table with Windows 10.

We can be certain, however, that BYOD will feature heavily in both Windows 10 and Windows Server 2016, as it's a crucial part of the business environment, with executives wanting to use their own iPad or sales staff only wanting to carry their own smartphone.

It's possible that much of the new BYOD functionality will be delayed until 2016 and the release of the next version of Windows Server. This was supposed to be released alongside Windows 10, however a delay was announced in late January 2015, perhaps because of bug and stability issues that Microsoft doesn't want to rush through.

Windows Server 2012 allows you to manage all manner of BYOD devices, and not just Windows PCs. These devices include both iOS and Android options. It's with Windows 8.1 devices, however, that the best BYOD experience is to be had, because they support features such as remote wipe, where a business can delete corporate data and files from the device remotely and at any time.

It's certain that we'll hear more about BYOD as 2015 progresses, and new and enhanced functionality that is centered on security will be forthcoming in Windows 10.

The Surface Hub

Microsoft's Surface brand has undergone a series of changes over the years. It began life back in 2007 as a 30-inch touchscreen table, intended for use in hotels and business spaces. It could interact with NFC tags attached to everyday objects and devices, and it used cameras to locate the user (or users), so that no matter where you sat at the table, the content you were viewing was always the correct way up.

The Surface name was transferred in 2012 to Microsoft's new tablet PCs, and it's for these devices that it's most widely and best known.

Large touch devices themselves became known as Microsoft PixelSense, such as the Microsoft/Samsung SUR40 table and Perceptive Pixel, which is better known as being the world's first 82-inch wall-mounted touch display.

Over the years I've had a chance to use both the original Microsoft Surface table and the Perceptive Pixel screen, and I've found both to be limiting, the former with a lack of useful applications, and the latter by a limiting 1080p resolution. It's clear, however, that large touchscreen devices *do* have a place in business, both in the boardroom as well as for business and political commentators on 24-hour news channels.

Thus, at Microsoft's January 2015 Windows 10 update event they introduced the world to the Surface Hub (see Figure 5-3).

Figure 5-3. *The Microsoft Surface Hub*

Surface Hub is a smart touchscreen device that will be available in 55-inch (1080p) and 84-inch (4K) versions. I say it's smart because it does much more than just work as a super-large touch screen. The Surface Hub has been designed as a "team device" that will help groups of people work together more effectively.

Digital Whiteboard

Probably the most obvious use for the Surface Hub is as a digital whiteboard, and it performs this job with a couple of pens (stored left and right on the screen's edges) and a specially-adapted version of OneNote.

Anybody in a meeting where a Surface Hub is being used who is also using a Windows 10 PC or phone can pair their device with the Surface Hub and automatically receive a copy of the meeting notes when the meeting is over.

Collaboration Tools

The Surface Hub comes equipped with cameras that help it perform a series of different tasks. One of these tasks to use the integrated Skype for Business app, which allows the Hub to be used for remote meetings.

Additionally, though, the Surface Hub can recognize individual people and wake up, welcome them, and log them in when they approach the device. The cameras can track movement and follow you as you move around the room. Also, anybody can share content from another Windows 10 device to the Surface Hub over the Miracast wireless display system, which is built into many modern laptops and tablets, including Microsoft's Surface Pro 3 and the Dell XPS 13 Ultrabook.

Specially-Designed Apps

Specially-created versions of Microsoft Office and other apps will be available for the Surface Hub, enabling groups of people to view and work collaboratively on files and documents together. The Surface Hub will use touch, ink, and sensors to allow third-party developers to create innovative collaboration apps and utilities for business.

Easy to Use and Deploy

The Surface Hub has been designed to be easy to use and deploy, requiring only a power lead and a Wi-Fi connection to get started. Microsoft will also be providing carts and stands so that the Hub can be moved easily from meeting room to meeting room.

Summary

It's clear that Windows 10 will bring a huge number of benefits, not just to home users and end users in the workplace, but also to business and system administrators.

The most important question still remains, however: How secure is it, both in everyday use and for business and remote workers? In the next chapter I'll detail the new and improved security features in Windows 10 and how they can be used in business and enterprise environments.

■ ■ ■

CHAPTER 6

Maximizing Security and Productivity

We're now living in a world where nothing is more crucial to a business than the security of its PCs and networks. On an all-too-often basis, we're hearing of hacks and data theft, often caused by simple username and password theft. These thefts include thousands, or even millions, of credit card and personal details. Private company emails are leaked to the Internet along with the Social Security numbers and bank details for employees.

In the face of such an onslaught it's perhaps tempting to retreat back into a purely offline world, but unless you keep all of your cash under your mattress and only spend it at the mall, that's impossible to do.

At your business you're likely responsible for the private details of others, and you're certainly responsible for your employees, not to mention confidential company documents. There is good news on the horizon, however, as Microsoft has always taken business security seriously. With Windows 10, they're filling in the gaps that have permitted attacks in the past.

Microsoft's Bitlocker full-drive encryption was the first major step toward securing our business files and data. It's so straightforward to use, robust, and scalable that I insist a Trusted Platform Module (TPM) chip comes with all the PCs I buy so as to securely store encryption keys.

This was made simpler with Windows 8.1, as all mobile devices were required to come with a TPM to qualify for the OS. But what's being added in Windows 10 to beef things up even further?

Security Features in Windows 8

Just as I wrote in Chapter 5, you may still be using Windows 7 on your PC(s) and might therefore be unaware of the security features that were introduced with Windows 8, and that will be carried forward into Windows 10.

This is a good starting point as, while Windows 8 received some bad press for being unfriendly for desktop users, there can be no doubt it's far more secure than its predecessor.

Application Sandboxing

Back in the days of Windows XP, access to files and system objects was controlled by simple access control lists (ACLs), which determined what users would have access to. Vista expanded on this functionality by introducing Protected Mode in Internet Explorer. This would run browser sessions in a sandboxed environment so that, for example, a website open in a browser or browser tab couldn't access memory or functions outside of that enclosed environment, which was sealed off from the rest of your OS and app functionality.

In Windows 8, AppContainers were introduced as a sandboxing method for new Windows Store apps. This extended this functionality, bringing it out of IE. All Windows 8 Universal apps would run in this sandboxed environment.

By default, each Windows 8 store app can only access its own storage area, and it has to declare its intention to access the user library, network, or device in its manifest file. These permissions are requested of the user and can be switched on and off in the app settings panel.

There are ten access areas that can be specified for apps.

- internetClient
- internetClientServer
- privateNetworkClientServer
- documentsLibrary
- picturesLibrary
- videosLibrary
- musicLibrary
- enterpriseAuthentication
- sharedUserCertificates
- removableStorage

In the business space, the *enterpriseAuthentication* permission allows apps to impersonate the credentials of the user when they are signed in to the company network so that the app can access features such as Azure or a domain.

Microsoft has said that they plan to extend this functionality in Windows 10, though at the time of writing new functionality has not yet been announced.

IE Enhanced Protected Mode

The sandboxed environment in Windows Vista was enhanced in Windows 8 with Enhanced Protected Mode (EPM). Each browser tab in the desktop version of Internet Explorer runs in its own sandboxed environment (the IE app already runs in a protected mode). EPM takes advantage of new security features such as Address Space Layout Randomization, which I will detail later in this chapter.

By default, EPM is disabled, though it can be forcibly activated through Group and Security Policies. It is disabled because there are some circumstances in which it could cause compatibility problems with company Intranet sites. It can be activated in the Internet Options section of the Control Panel (see Figure 6-1).

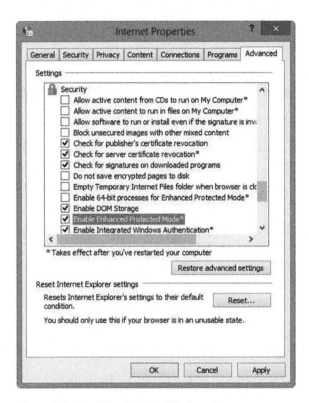

Figure 6-1. *Enabling EPM in Windows 8*

Advanced Exploit Protection

This protected mode includes new security features, including Address Space Layout Randomization (ASLR), which randomizes the location of system libraries in the OS, thus making a malware attack more difficult. Although first introduced in Vista, this feature was enhanced in Windows 8 to include randomization of DLL (Dynamic Link Library) locations that weren't previously compatible with the ASLR feature.

Intel Secure Key Technology is a random number generator that provides improved security when relying on the system clock. It works by randomizing some low-level memory allocation functions, which in turn randomizes the addresses for system libraries as well as apps, including win32 desktop programs.

Additionally, the Windows 8 operating system kernel runs in its own non-executable, protected memory area, sandboxing it and making it harder to attack. Intel's Supervisor Mode Execution Prevention (SMEP), which was introduced with their Ivy Bridge Core processors, improves this security further by making it more difficult for malware to exploit any bugs that may exist in the kernel files. It does this by not allowing the kernel to execute code that resides in memory, where malware tends to hide.

SmartScreen

Website integrity checking is nothing new for browsers, but for the first time Windows 8 included it baked into the OS. SmartScreen not only checks websites against white and black lists held and maintained by Microsoft and other security companies, but also checks downloaded files and apps.

It's a very effective method for protecting a PC from malware and is, by default, set to require administrator-level authentication before a suspect package can be open or run.

Secure Boot

One of the most talked-about security features when Windows 8 was launched was secure boot. This is a system built into the EFI protocols that verifies the integrity of bootable operating system files, thus preventing the injection and execution of malware into the boot systems of an OS.

Secure Boot gained notoriety because it was supported by Windows 8, and indeed it was made a requirement for all Original Equipment Manufacturers (OEMs) distributing new PCs; however, it wasn't supported by GNU/Linux operating systems.

Secure Boot could be disabled in the PC's EFI system, though not all OEMs would support disabling the feature, making it impossible to dual-boot some systems with a non-digitally-signed OS.

When Windows is installed, the OS creates an authentication key that is used to verify the integrity of the OS at boot time. Malware and rootkits that attempt to modify the boot loader system would require changes be made to the authentication key in order to enable themselves to load. This key, however, is protected by the EFI system and cannot be altered.

An additional function that Microsoft introduced to help bolster the Secure Boot system is called Early Launch Anti-Malware (ELAM). This enables compatible security suites to load early in the Windows boot sequence, therefore offering malware protection throughout the boot sequence, rather loading security suites only after an infected OS may have already displayed the desktop.

■ **Note** You can confirm whether SecureBoot is configured and running for your installed copy of Windows by opening a PowerShell window with administrator privileges and typing the command **confirm-SecureBootUEFI**.

Windows 8 loads its ELAM driver first, which allows anti-virus software to identify at boot time if subsequent drivers should be initialized. ELAM is not configured by default but can be activated in Group Policy by searching for *Computer Configuration, Administrative Templates, System, Early Launch Anti-Malware* (see Figure 6-2).

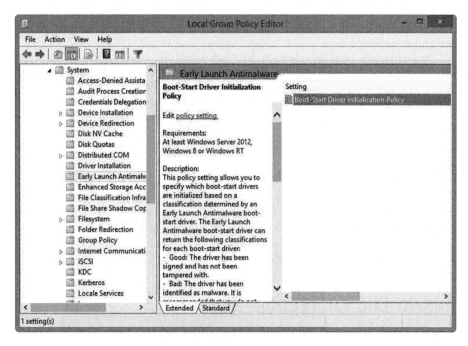

Figure 6-2. *Enabling ELAM in Group Policy*

If your PC comes with a TPM chip, it has the new MeasuredBoot system, which was introduced to allow antivirus software vendors to verify the health of PCs through the use of a log file stored on the TPM chip itself.

This log can be used to verify the integrity of drivers and Windows components that are loaded before the anti-virus engine starts. After boot, the anti-virus software can check the log file to see if any files or components have been altered.

Two-Factor Authentication in the OS

The biggest security flaw with any PC is the soft, squidgy thing at the keyboard. The vast majority of computer hacks come from obtaining the usernames and password of employees who seem, all too often, eager and willing to provide them to anybody who phones claiming to be tech support, or who sends an email that's apparently from their bank.

Clearly this flaw had to be plugged, and strong passwords alone were never going to do it. Windows 10 bakes two-factor authentication right into the OS and gives us a few ways to use it, adding valuable flexibility for businesses. We've had smartcard authentication for years already, but Windows 10 takes this a step further by beefing up its biometric support, enabling PC systems to require access to fingerprint or other unique data.

Even better is the ability to use another Windows device, such as a smartphone, to act as a two-factor authentication device over Bluetooth or Wi-Fi. This feature means that both a laptop and phone would have to be stolen together in order for a thief to gain access to the PC, and additionally they'd need the unlock code for the phone before the authentication would work.

An employee leaving their office PC for lunch would also no longer have to worry about security for the time they're absent from their desk. Removing the phone from the vicinity of the PC will automatically trigger the locking of the PC.

This new two-factor authentication feature will also be supported by Azure and Active Directory when Windows 10 launches, along with Microsoft Accounts, which are also including the feature.

User Access Token Protection

Even two-factor authentication systems can be breached if an attacker is able to obtain the User Access Token, however. With Windows 10, Microsoft is storing the UAT's insecure containers, which are built on top of Hyper-V technology.

This new security measure will prevent the UATs from being extracted, even if the Windows kernel is itself compromised with malware.

End-to-End Encryption

A weak point for business security is always the transfer of data or files across a network or Internet connection, whether protected by a Virtual Private Network or not. With Windows 10, Microsoft is adding end-to-end encryption for corporate apps, data, email, and website traffic.

The data to be protected with this method can be specified by corporate security policies, and this includes a blanket coverage of all data transfers, should you wish to turn that feature on.

Encryption will happen seamlessly and transparently without the user having to get involved. This functionality will also extend to smartphones running Windows 10. Businesses will be able to configure this encryption in such a way that it happens automatically for all network traffic.

App Protection

Additionally, businesses will be able to define which apps can and should have access to corporate data. Using security and group policy controls, only approved apps and app versions will have access to company data through VPN connections.

This functionality will extend both to desktop (win32) and Universal apps, so you can feel assured that you're covered and that your data will be safe.

Additionally, BYOD policies will enable system administrators to specify that only trusted apps can be installed on devices that access company data. This again includes win32 and Universal apps.

Threat Resistance

I've written a lot about Windows Troubleshooting over the last few years, and one of the themes I keep coming back to is that the biggest weak point in the security of any PC is the soft, squidgy thing at the keyboard.

It's not that computer users are in any way stupid or naïve; it's that the days of a virus being transferred on a removable disc or in a Word file macro are (almost) long gone.

Nowadays, the trick is in deceiving the user, and cyber-criminals are very deft at this. Despite the fact that our operating systems and apps have become much easier to use, with tablet operating systems such as iOS and Windows Metro lowering the bar to entry, they are still very complex underneath.

This leads to many weak points that can be attacked, and the effectiveness of those attacks boils down to how you exploit the user.

In many instances, these attacks will involve a user being phoned and asked for their password by "IT Support." Windows 10 brings the two-factor authentication enhancements I mentioned earlier in this chapter to help combat this. But what happens if a user is tricked into clicking something they shouldn't have, and that action results in malware being installed on the PC?

With Windows 10, organizations will be able to use new threat-resistance tools to lock down PCs, only allowing them to install trusted apps (and only trusted versions of those apps). Apps will be digitally signed by Microsoft to certify their authenticity, and OEMs (Original Equipment Manufacturers) and organizations will be able to submit their own apps for vetting and certification.

This certification for apps isn't just for Universal apps either. Microsoft has said that win32 desktop programs can be submitted for certification and trusted by organizations in the same way as company store apps.

Summary

While we will have to wait until sometime in 2016 for the next version of Windows Server, which will bring more and better security functionality to the Windows 10 desktop, there can be little doubt that the security enhancements in Microsoft's new OS represent a great leap forward.

Having an operating system where all communication is encrypted by default, and where a phone or biometric device can be used with a PC as a two-factor authentication device, will reassure many IT Pros.

Add to this the additional sandboxing for the OS and applications and stricter controls for BYOD PCs, and Windows 10 will present a serious challenge for any cyber-criminal or malware writer.

I sincerely hope you've found this book useful in giving you a full, in-depth overview of Microsoft's new Windows 10 operating system. The benefits for organizations and end-users are substantial, and the consumer pricing is compelling. Will you be upgrading?

Index

Get the eBook for only $10!

> Now you can take the weightless companion with you anywhere, anytime. Your purchase of this book entitles you to 3 electronic versions for only $10.

This Apress title will prove so indispensible that you'll want to carry it with you everywhere, which is why we are offering the eBook in 3 formats for only $10 if you have already purchased the print book.

Convenient and fully searchable, the PDF version enables you to easily find and copy code—or perform examples by quickly toggling between instructions and applications. The MOBI format is ideal for your Kindle, while the ePUB can be utilized on a variety of mobile devices.

Go to www.apress.com/promo/tendollars to purchase your companion eBook.

Apress®
THE EXPERT'S VOICE™

Printed by Printforce, the Netherlands